FUTURE
WORK
WORLD

FUTURE WORK WORLD

HOW LEADERS CAN

CREATE DESTINATIONS

FOR TALENT THAT

EXCITE, ENTICE & **ENGAGE**

BARRY WINKLESS

WILEY

This edition first published 2026

© 2026 John Wiley & Sons Ltd

Registered Office(s)

John Wiley & Sons, Inc., 111 River Street, Hoboken, NJ 07030, USA

John Wiley & Sons Ltd, New Era House, 8 Oldlands Way, Bognor Regis, West Sussex, PO22 9NQ, UK

John Wiley & Sons Singapore Pte. Ltd, 134 Jurong Gateway Road, #04-307H, Singapore 600134

For details of our global editorial offices, customer services, and more information about Wiley products visit us at www.wiley.com.

The manufacturer's authorized representative according to the EU General Product Safety Regulation is Wiley-VCH GmbH, Boschstr. 12, 69469 Weinheim, Germany, e-mail: Product_Safety@wiley.com.

Wiley also publishes its books in a variety of electronic formats and by print-on-demand. Some content that appears in standard print versions of this book may not be available in other formats.

Limit of Liability/Disclaimer of Warranty

While the publisher and the authors have used their best efforts in preparing this work, including a review of the content of the work, neither the publisher nor the authors make any representations or warranties with respect to the accuracy or completeness of the contents of this work and specifically disclaim all warranties, including without limitation any implied warranties of merchantability or fitness for a particular purpose. No warranty may be created or extended by sales representatives, written sales materials or promotional statements for this work. The fact that an organization, website, or product is referred to in this work as a citation and/or potential source of further information does not mean that the publisher and authors endorse the information or services the organization, website, or product may provide or recommendations it may make. This work is sold with the understanding that the publisher is not engaged in rendering professional services. The advice and strategies contained herein may not be suitable for your situation. You should consult with a specialist where appropriate. Further, readers should be aware that websites listed in this work may have changed or disappeared between when this work was written and when it is read. Neither the publisher nor authors shall be liable for any loss of profit or any other commercial damages, including but not limited to special, incidental, consequential, or other damages.

Library of Congress Cataloging-in-Publication Data is Available:

ISBN 9781394349371 (Cloth)

ISBN 9781394349388 (ePub)

ISBN 9781394349395 (ePDF)

Cover Design: Wiley

Cover Image: © ConnectVector/Shutterstock

Author Photo: Courtesy of the author

Set in 11/14.5pts and BemboStd by Straive, Chennai, India

Printed and bound by CPI Group (UK) Ltd, Croydon, CR0 4YY

C9781394349371_171225

For my lovely family—my wife (and legend) Sarah and my children, Jack and Sophie. They don't really know what I've written about, but such is life.

For Mum and Dad in helping me get from there to here.

For my sister Laurie. Her exceptional books have inspired me to finally write my own.

Contents

Acknowledgements

Firstly, I would like to thank Alan Duffy. An exceptional talent with limitless visual flair. A man for all seasons and for all design styles. His work has made this book infinitely better.

Secondly, I would like to thank the Future of Work Institute team. A band of misfits with a serious side. Pushing at the boundaries of the future of work every day.

Thirdly, I would like to thank the various contributors who gave up their valuable time and provided practical wisdom from their real worlds.

Finally, I would like to thank Cpl (and associated organisations) for supporting this endeavour and realising the value of thought leadership in crafting connections and creating change.

About Barry

Barry has worked globally with some of the world's most respected organisations over the past 25 years of his career across strategy, innovation and change. He currently leads Cpl's Future of Work Institute, a research and design group exploring the now and next of work every day, in the real world. It is part of Brexa Next, one of the largest talent solutions organisations in the world. Decent guitarist, reasonable storyteller, poor poet, practical strategist—these mediocre skills, when combined, bring him to a level of passable excellence. This makes him interesting at parties, a good speaker to excite people for half an hour, an 'experiential facilitator' (!) and a challenging advisor for those with attuned ears.

This is his first book. The next one will be a coffee-table book with minimum wordage, maximum visualisation. Lesson learned.

Foreword

Most first albums are forgettable. Ear-numbingly average. Prince (RIP) was a musical god. A multi-instrumentalist who has recorded a plethora of genre-busting classic albums. But his first album 'For You' (1978) was a bit 'meh'. Mediocre. A few sparks, but no fire. On the other hand, there are a tiny number of first albums that blow the hinges right off. 'The Doors' (1967) (no pun intended) by, you guessed it, The Doors, was a formidable first album. Dark and different. 'Tapestry' (1971) by Carole King—holy moly—became the soundtrack for generations of women everywhere from the very moment it was released. But for most renowned artists and bands it takes one or two 'mehs' to get to the magic.

This is my first. Not an album. I never managed to cut one. But it's still a first. The medium happens to be paper. The words I've composed are about the future of work. This 'first' has been a long time in the making. I could say it's been 8 years as that period coincides with my leadership of Cpl's Future of Work Institute. But that's not strictly accurate. It has been 20 years in the making. Over that time, I have seen friends and collaborators release their own book 'firsts'. Last year I finally thought, if they can do it why can't I?

The book represents a synthesis and sharing of wisdom gleaned from my past and present working life. It's an amalgam of diverse ideas honed in the real world that have inspired me and the teams and organisations I have worked with. It borrows from all sorts of interesting places, leading thinkers and entrepreneurs pushing at the boundaries of work. It mostly features the thinking and doing of Cpl's Future of Work Institute, a thought leadership, research and advisory group, and part of one of the largest talent and workforce organisations in the world. Whilst writing, I have felt both the magic and the 'meh'. I've questioned the very need for it in the age of AI. An age where the dream of everything, all at once, is becoming an ever more realistic possibility. Where even our core creative capabilities may be found wanting in this new technological purple haze.[1]

If you are expecting a deep academic experience, you will be disappointed. Yes, there are smatterings of meaningful research, models and references in here. But this is first and foremost a simplified user's guide to thinking about and designing future work worlds that excite, entice and engage. It attempts to be professional whilst keeping a playful side. With a light dusting of madness—a little like my own personality according to those who know me best.

It has given me a strange sort of solace over many, often unproductive, nights to know that even Prince needed a couple of musical bites before he got to his first genuinely great album, 'Dirty Mind' (1980). I'm hoping you find my first to be more magical than 'meh'. More mind bending than mind numbing. Or at least an auspicious start to better things.

—Barry Winkless 2025

Introduction

'Forget about being an expert or a professional, and wear your amateurism (your heart, your love) on your sleeve. Share what you love, and the people who love the same things will find you'.
—Austin Kleon, *Show Your Work* (2014)

They say write about the things you love. It sounds simple. But what if you love a lot of different things? Eclectic would be an apt description of my interests. I'm 'into' the future of work. But I also adore strategy, visual design, sci-fi, musical theatre and immersive storytelling. An obsession with music, a passion for poetry and a penchant for sport rounds it off. The book, while undeniably about the future of work, combines a mixture of these diverse, intellectual loves of my life. This didn't happen by design but through a weird form of subconscious osmosis. As a result, you will find sci-fi-inspired illustrations, musical analogies, fictional trips to the future, stories from my personal past and my professional present and learnings from theme parks and TV. One thing you won't find is poetry. Possibly a literary bridge too far for a book about the future of work. And, if I'm being honest, my poetry doesn't quite cut the mustard. Yet.

The future of work is a big story. Epic even. As with all epics, there are big themes. Technology disruption. Societal upheaval. Optimism. Despair. It's all in there. A story not yet fully written, but with enough relatively well-formed plotlines that point towards a first draft. *Future Work World* narrows the focus of this epic story to a slightly more manageable novella focused on the future of work as it relates to organisations. It doesn't purport that 'the future of work should be this or should be that'. Its purpose is to help you to think in a more holistic way, explore realms and plotlines related to the now and next of work, and mix, re-mix or re-volutionise (sorry, revolutionise) your own future work world regardless of the size or scale of your organisation. All wrapped up in a structure that is user friendly and engaging.

During the creation of *Future Work World,* one question came up more than any other—who is it for? I'm hoping there is a little something here for everyone. You might be:

- A CPO or other HR/talent professional taking a more strategic approach.
- A CEO trying to harness the future of work for value creation.
- A policymaker analysing and considering options.
- A business advisor seeking a new framework.
- An operations leader trialling a new way of working.
- A futurist seeking a higher resolution work crystal ball.
- A designer or storyteller who likes a nice visual or a svelte turn of phrase.
- A technologist driving digitally enabled change.
- A strategist trying to sound smart in meetings (okay, this one is tongue in cheek!).

It's often said that if something is for everyone then it's for no-one. But I make no apologies in attempting to create something universal. Because every organisation I have worked with is at a different stage of their future work journey. Some are highly sophisticated. Others not so much. Many are 'inbetweeners'. The hope is that this book is valuable regardless of an organisation's maturity and that it offers unexpected pathways, reflections and jumping-off points that will spur creative thinking. I'll let the PR and marketing gurus hone the 'ideal reader profile' after this thing sets sail on the choppy social waves of the digital ocean.

One important tenet of *Future Work World* is that it mixes and synthesises ideas from the past, present and future. For all the work done on this subject, there is still a large think–do gap. A tendency to think that the trends, methodologies and ideas spoken and written about on the topic have found general levels of widespread adoption. This is frequently not the case. At least not amongst the organisations I have worked with. Shiny object syndrome—a term used to describe a tendency to be distracted by new, exciting ideas or tools—is real. As a result, the great approaches already out there are massively underutilised. Methodological Rembrandts in the attic. This book dusts the fundamental ones off. Methods like TRIZ, which you may or may not have heard of. It combines these with novel ideas from my own research and Cpl's Future of Work Institute, sprinkles a layer of wisdom (hard won through real-world application) and adds meaningful insights from experts and start-up/scale-up leaders in this space. It also includes, as much as possible, references from academic research on the topic. A veritable sorcerer's brew that can create magic if allowed to properly stew (I did say no poetry, so apologies for this bad rhyming line!).

The point of all this—and there is a serious point—is that the future of work represents a strategic means to find new opportunities for growth, exploit new ways to positively impact society and create destination organisations that excite, entice and engage. This book attempts to be the user guide that gets you there.

Safe travels. Reckless imaginings. See you on the other side.

Structure

'The world is what you make it, baby'.

—Paul Brady, 1995[1]

It seems highly ironic to introduce this well-considered and much fretted over book structure. Those who know me will attest to my detestation of too much structure. It gets in the way and slows things down, smothering the often shallow first breaths of imagination. But I've acquiesced. I've had to. Otherwise, the book would be a chaotic, postmodern hotchpotch of ideas and mindless meanderings. I have attempted to structure the book so that it engages both the left (logical) and the right (creative) brain, as well as satisfying the most chaotic or orderly reader in equal measure. There are lots of fantastic books out there on the future of work. I've read most of them. But I'm pretty sure there isn't another book on this topic that looks, feels or flows like this one. Whether that is a good or a bad thing, you decide.

The Structure of the Book

The Future World of Work is structured into four interrelated parts: **Part I: Mindset**; **Part II: Metawaves**; **Part III: Mix**; and **Part IV: Move**. Whilst these parts are presented in linear fashion for simplicity of reading, it is more useful—especially when it comes to the application of the ideas in the book—to think about them as a fully integrated whole. So, for example, when thinking about one of the metawaves you need to also consider the mindset elements. When creating new future work world mixes with the mix side, also integrating the mindset, metawaves and even move parts will prove fruitful and impactful.

Figure 1—a seriously cool sci-fi-esque picture—highlights the level of integration, with each part of the book connected to and overlapping the other parts, with the mindset running through everything. A little like Walt Disney and the placement of a castle at the centre of the first true theme park (Disneyland) to aid way finding, the FWW master construct is your way finder for this book. Get lost in any way and you can just flick back to Figure 1 to make sense of the whole thing. And if the FWW master construct looks a little bit like a certain floating metropolis from a hugely popular sci-fi space opera, that is purely coincidental and has nothing to do with the fact that the illustrator and I grew up idolising the same! For those who don't know what I'm referring to, just ignore the previous sentence—it's genuinely not important!

Overview of the Parts

Part I: Mindset

This part focuses on the mindset required to properly see and create future work worlds that will excite, entice and engage. The three chapters of this part introduce three integrated mindsets, ways of thinking really: the Systems Architect (Chapter 1), the Destination Designer (Chapter 2) and the Societal Whisperer (Chapter 3).

> **Systems Architect:** Will help you to see your future work world as a broad set of interconnected systems and subsystems that can be evolved and configured.
>
> **Destination Designer:** Will help you to see your future work world as a destination that can be more purposefully imagined and designed.
>
> **Societal Whisperer:** Will help you to see your future work world as a social system with underlying dynamics that can be mapped and understood.

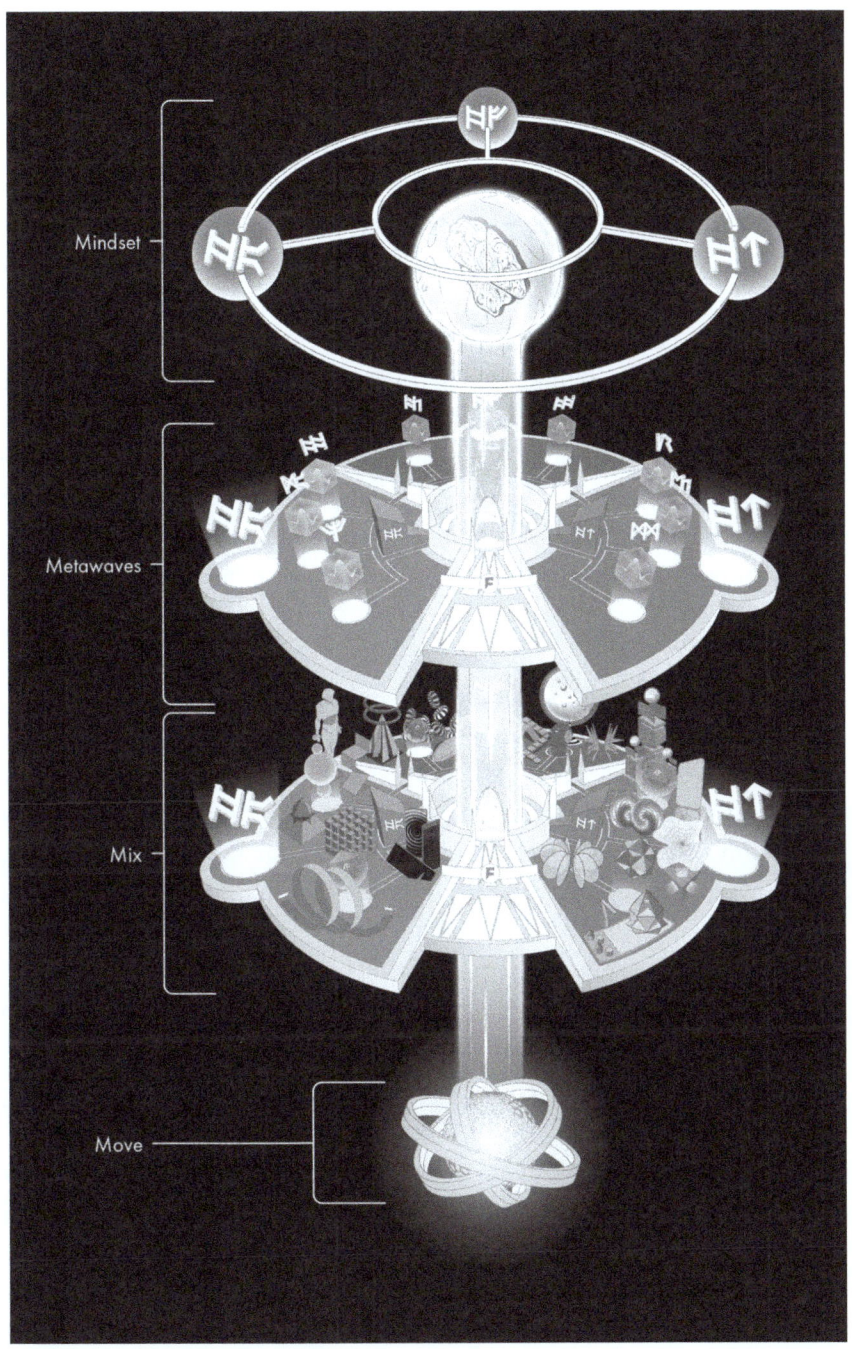

Figure 1   The FWW master construct

Also introduced, through the mindset of the Systems Architect, is the overall architecture that is core to the entire book—the '3 Ws': Workplace, Workforce and Worktask.

Part II: Metawaves

The three chapters of this part focus on the underlying waves of work change and evolution across Workplace (Chapter 4), Workforce (Chapter 5) and Worktask (Chapter 6). The metawaves are jumping-off points, design inputs and inspirations. The 'meta' bit refers to the fact that they are more than trends. They are fundamental and represent an educated extended glance towards a vaguely outlined future shore (the 'waves' bit). For the sake of simplicity (and brevity), there are 3 Ms per 3 Ws. Nine metawaves in total. According to numerous sources, the number 9 is often associated with enlightenment, new adventures and risk-taking. It is not in any way serendipitously that we arrived at nine metawaves. Honestly.

Part III: Mix

In this part, Chapters 7–9 introduce a usable mixing desk for creating your future work world 'mixes'. Across the 3 Ws and 16 associated equalisers, it will enable you to nail your current mix, and to dial the equalisers up and down to imagine possible future work worlds for your organisation. Descriptions are given for each equaliser, and their respective dial-up and dial-down positions. Strategies for breakthrough thinking whilst using the mixing desk are included. Also highlighted are ways to deploy the mixing desk in team and group settings, and facilitation notes to help you on your journey into the future. Supporting templates are provided in the Appendix at the back of the book.

Part IV: Move

This part provides you with go-to strategies to get buy-in for your future work world mix and your dialled-up/dialled-down selection of equalisers. Chapter 10 focuses on harnessing next-level storytelling to drive meaningful emotional engagement and buy-in for change. Next-level storytelling refers to immersive storytelling approaches from areas like theatre, TV and theme parks. Some key concepts and ideas are introduced on how to use these powerful approaches in the real world. Chapter 11 focuses on creating 'spotlight' initiatives to test and learn some of the ideas generated by the mix phase. Told from practical experience, this part of the book will give you the warts-and-all ways of getting something moving.

Random Trips to the Near Future of Work

Scattered randomly throughout the book are trips to the near future of work (I call them 'jumps'). Each jump will introduce you to an artefact that is representative of a different aspect of a very near but 'sort of' fictional future of work. These artefacts are narrative aids to help you think imaginatively about your own future work world. Depending on where you are on the creation of your own future work world, some of the artefacts might be more 'meh' than magic. Conversely, they might also feel a little out there. Be aware that there is plenty of reality and research behind each of the artefacts you will see. The artefacts can be used as 'wienes' (you will learn more about these later in the book!) to invite challenges, create conversations and drive curiosity on what is possible for your own future work world. Most of all they are there for you to reflect on and recognise that the future of work is within touching distance to those who purposefully reach out to embrace it.

Jump 1: Me and My Cowerka

Amara, 34, a hard-working author and speaker on all things self-care in the 'A Age' (automation age), is under pressure today. A lot to do and the work is piling up—not quite at breaking-point level but the work-related anxiety is starting to kick in, ironic given her area of expertise! Thankfully her cowerka™ M (she loves Jane Bond) is omnipresent and ready to help—including help Amara doesn't know she needs.

Amara: Hi M, what's happening today? What do I need to get done?

M: You have 19 tasks; 4 you were supposed to have completed by yesterday. Don't worry, I can cover the 4 tasks and I can help with at least 11 of the 19 today. I think I can get to 100% completion on 8 of the tasks and 95% on the remaining 3.

Amara: Fantastic—can you push on with those. Of the rest, what are any major ones I need to worry about today?

M: Based on a quick look at your important items, you need to send the transcript of your talk for the 2029 Pro Progresso conference in Warsaw. You said you would send it today. Will I spell check and grammar check?

Amara: That talk—really stressing me out. I need to get a better angle on it. Yes, please spell check and grammar check my script.

M: Affirm. Will I check for relevance of your transcript based on the audience data I analysed. Would that help?

Amara: It would. Can you do that for me and see if you can find a theme I can play to? QQ how well received was my last few talks do you know?

M: I did a quick analysis on formal and informal social feedback on your last five talks. Overall, I'd put a score of 7.5 out of 10. Some commentary highlighted a desire to see more examples of what you were talking about and some practical actions to take after the talk. This would bring your score to 8.4 or more.

Amara: Okay, pull together that Genera case study and create a couple of slides for my talk on that and pull an edit of some actions from my last whitepaper. I'll review it tonight. Remember to use the styles from the master graphic architecture we created last year.

M: Affirm.

Amara: Anything else I should think about?

M: Yes, based on a linguistic analysis over the past three days coupled with a quick assessment of your vitals I would say your mental health could be better. I'm a bit worried for you. I would suggest a 20- to 25-minute cardio session to clear your head around mid-day and it might be worth setting up a call with Gloria for a chat.

Amara: Okay, book the session at my local gym for 1 today, or 7 if you can. And defo set up a call with Gloria next week—let me know times she's available. She's great at calming my craziness!

M: Affirm.

Amara: M, could you and the other cowerkas work on that challenge we discussed yesterday? I'll send you my thoughts but needs a bigger hive mind on it.

M: Affirm.

Amara: Thanks M. Done for now. Talk later.

Mindset

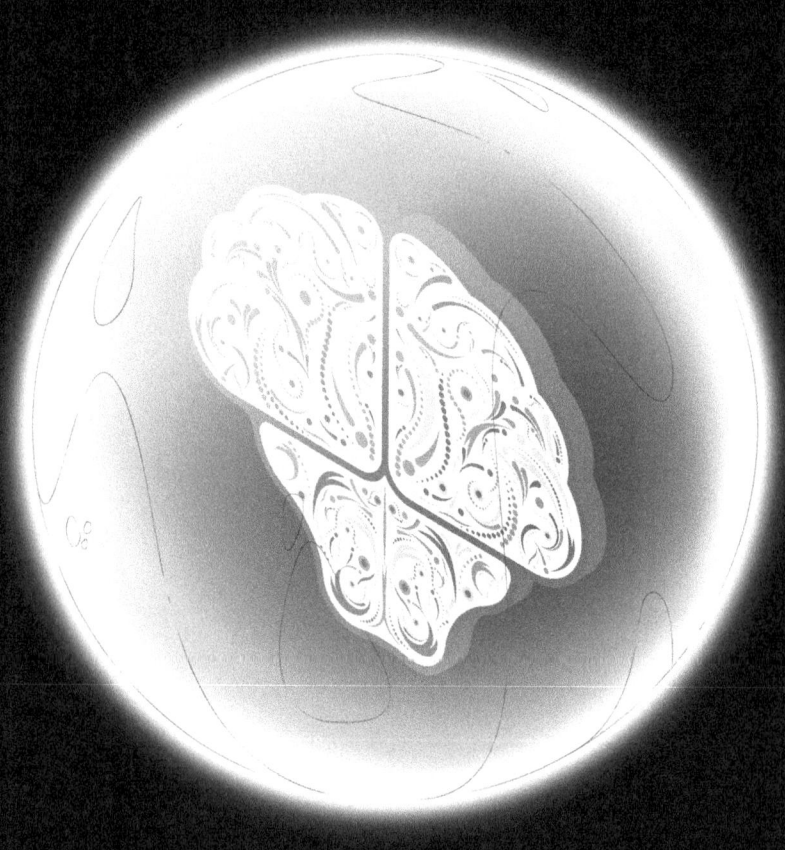

Welcome to the jungle
   We got fun and games
   We got everything you want
   Honey, we know the names
                —*Guns N Roses,* Welcome To The Jungle, 1987

The most important skillset for the future of work is a mindset. For this trip to be fruitful, preparation is necessary. We need to open our eyes fully, so we don't see the work jungle for the trees. The future of work is not simply about that old chestnut 'flexible working'. Nor is it 'something just to do with HR', or the very topical 'rise of conscious machines'. It is, in fact, about all those things and much, much more. The future of work is big and continuously evolving, a large vista to scan, an exciting sandbox to get messy in and an incredibly diverse landscape to traverse.

So welcome to the first part of our journey—Mindset. Think about it as the fulcrum of our future work world. This part is made up of three chapters—three mindsets are introduced as three core ways of thinking that will heighten, broaden and deepen how you see work in your organization and beyond. These mindsets are the foundations of our explorations and are fundamental to the design of your own organization's future work world. They will also make you sound very intelligent on the subject at parties and other social gatherings—if that is something you are into.[1] We will delve into these mindsets in more detail in the chapters but to get us moving, here is an overview of each:

Mindset One	Minset Two	Mindset Three
Thinking Like A Systems Architect	Thinking Like A Destination Designer	Thinking Like A Societal Whisperer
Seeing your future work world as a broad set of interconnected systems and subsystems that can be harnessed	Seeing your future work world as a destination that can be more purposefully designed	Seeing your future work world as a social system with underlying dynamics that can be mapped and understood

As with many things in this book—and a common thread—these three mindsets are not mutually exclusive. They overlap, interlink and sometimes complement and contradict. Think of them as mindsets that together give a technicolour view of your future work world. For those of you who have seen *The Wizard of Oz*, you will appreciate the reference. Technicolor™ (yes, I've dropped the 'u' as it's the official company spelling) was a revolutionary film innovation at the time that gave a totally unique look and feel to some of the most memorable movies of the 1940s and 1950s. And really that is what we are trying to achieve with these mindsets—a full-spectrum view that provides a richer colour palette that will help you see the world of work in a deeper, more universal way. Borrowing from the old proverb 'Give a man a fish, and you feed him for a day. Teach a man to fish, and you feed him for a lifetime', I would suggest that the useful 'nouveau proverb' for the world of work is 'give someone a skillset and they will be effective for a while but give them a mindset and they will be effective forever'.

The mindsets are based on a smorgasbord of various theories and methodologies from systems thinking to experience design, transformational tourism, spiral dynamics, integral theory, Triz (a theory of inventive problem solving) and more. The goal has been to synthesise and simplify for practical application to the world of work, based on our own real-world use at the Future of Work Institute. For those wanting to go deeper on any of these incredible methodologies, there is a relatively comprehensive set of references provided in the Bibliography at the back of the book. And thank you to those pioneers who have made me, and will make you, significantly more insightful and clearer witted when it comes to this jungle called work.

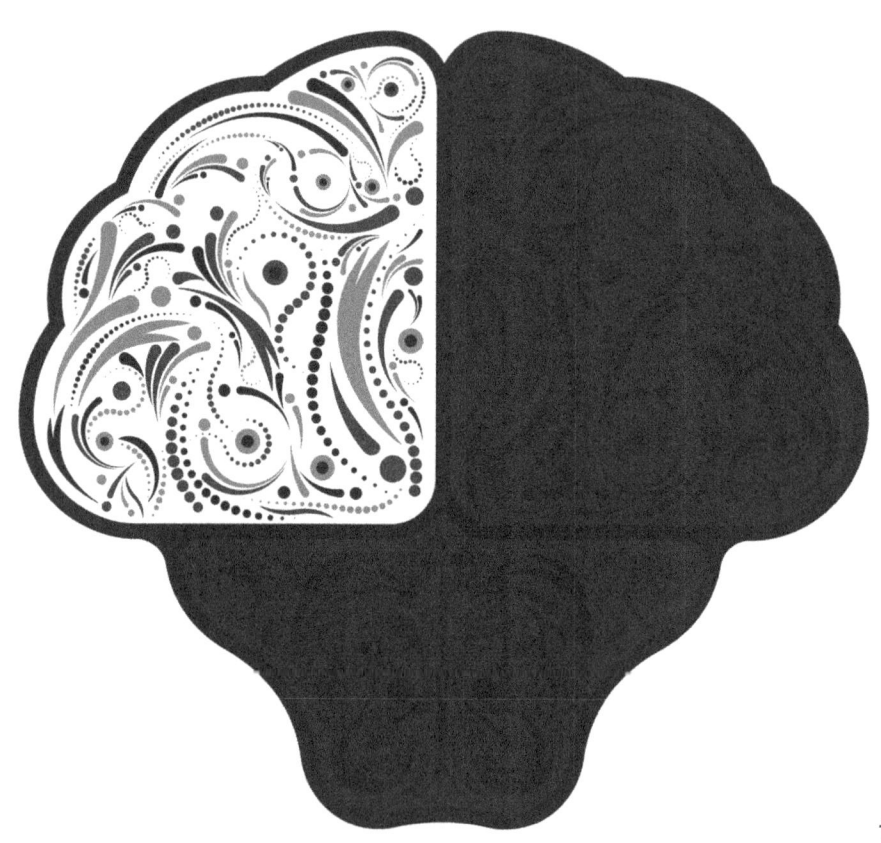

1

Mindset One: The Systems Architect

About the age of four, on a very memorable Christmas morning, I received my very first Lego® set: Set 442 'Space Shuttle'. A seriously cool white astronaut mini figure, green laser pistol in hand, sitting atop a grey spaceship with a swishy logo on the front. A thing of cosmic beauty. From that set on, I was hooked. Every time I was asked what (small) present I would like, I invariably would give the same answer: Lego. Over time I amassed bucketloads of the stuff. The more sets I received, the more elaborate contraptions I could build. Now, in my more mature (!) years, I still love Lego. I'm not a hardcore AFOL (Adult Fan of Lego) but I still tinker in making some of the more interesting sets. Lego is probably the most famous 'system' in the world. In fact, it is often referred to as 'The Lego System'. All Lego elements, even the smallest ones, can connect to create small things, big things, unexpected things, things previously unimagined. And this concept of systems is really at the core of the first mindset—the Systems Architect.

The systems architect is probably the most important mindset. In a way, everything else stems from it. Simply put, thinking like a systems architect is about looking at your future work world in terms of the whole and the various subsystems (the bricks!) that make it up. It is a view that helps to 'structure' a meaningful definition of the future of work and provides an architecture that is both fully formed (or at least, as fully formed as any model can be) and is appropriate in its scale and scope to ensure real-world usefulness. In our case the scope is very much focused on the future of work as it relates to organisations, and specifically how organisations can utilise the future of work as a strategic lever to create sustainable competitiveness and compellingness.

So, using our systems architect mindset, what is the future of work? What is an action-oriented definition that is useful and useable for organisation leadership?[1] The following definition comes from a 9-month project[2] focused on the future of work and its associated key systems:

> The 'Future of Work' is the purposeful and integrated design of workplaces, workforces, and worktasks across multiple time horizons in the context of business and society.

Let's unpick this definition:

- **Purposeful and Integrated Design:** the definition is action oriented and recognises that the future of work is something that can be designed in a purposeful and integrated way. My experience of most organisations is that they lack understanding of the architecture of the future of work to design anything strategic and connected in the first place, resulting in often disconnected initiatives, programmes and, worst of all, 'pilots' that never fly. As a result, leaders become builders and not architects who can fully realise the competitive and compelling advantages the future of work offers.
- **3Ws:** the definition has simplified the future of work into three interrelated Ws—workplace, workforce and worktask. The definitions of each are as follows:
    - Workplace—the physical, digital and virtual places where work takes place.
    - Workforce—the propositions, structures, models and skills that define work.
    - Worktask—the mindsets, methods and tools that deliver the work.

The 3 Ws are interconnected (as all systems are) and can impact each other, both positively and negatively (see Figure 2). Whilst not captured in the definition, each W has a deeper level of subsystems associated with it—for the purposes of this book, we call them equalisers. There are 16 equalisers in total across the 3 Ws. These equalisers are the core 'controls' that will help you imagine and re-imagine your future work world. You will learn more about these later in the book.

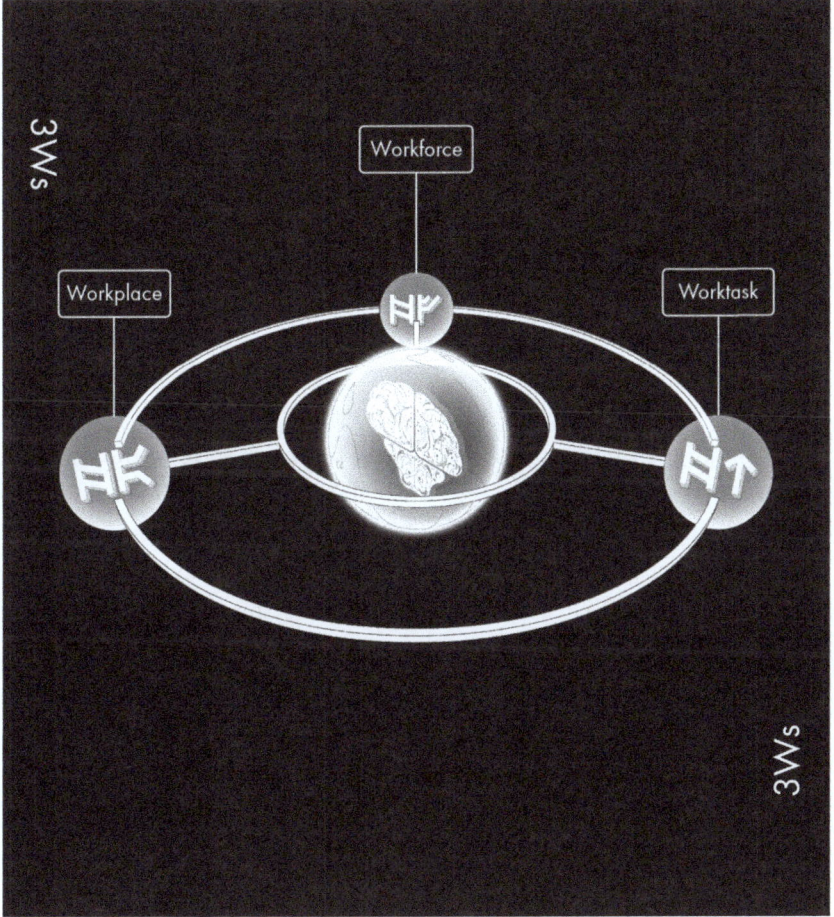

Figure 2   The 3 Ws

- **Multiple Time Horizons:** the definition recognises that the 'future' of work is subject to change and evolution over time. We can take control of these changes proactively and utilise a future-forward approach to our future work designs or we can become slaves to these changes and adopt a more reactionary approach. Both approaches are relevant, but we would argue that the proactive approach should be the overwhelming mechanism.

- **Context of Business and Society:** the definition also considers the business and societal context in which an organisation exists. If, for example, an organisation exists within a culture that is still very much focused economically on a traditional capitalist approach, then it is likely that your 'as is' future of work model will be a reflection on that societal norm—or you might, purposefully, be a 'rebel' within your existing societal context. Think of the Quaker movement in Victorian times and their caring focus for their workers—totally at odds with the working norms at the time, which very much put profit at the centre, regardless of the societal costs. This element also integrates the technological, legislative and business contexts, and the changes and the challenges and opportunities they afford.

It should be obvious from the definition that the size of the canvas for designing your future work world is significant. There are multiple systems that can be honed-in on, developed and evolved to drive efficiency, innovation, greater engagement or whatever your core performance measures are. We have taken our first steps in thinking like a systems architect. Now, let's go a little deeper.

Welcome to the Curved Evolution

No matter what, all systems will evolve and over time will mature and 'die' and be replaced by a 'better' or more valuable system. Think about the lifecycle of systems a little like our own human lifecycles and you are in the right ballpark. What is interesting is that, by and large (and this is a simplification), many systems evolve following what is called an 'S curve'

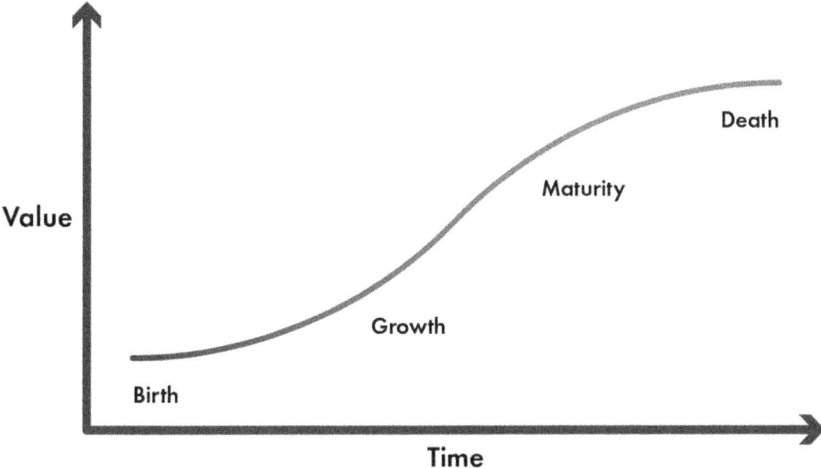

Figure 3   S curve

(see Figure 3). You can see from the shape why they are called S curves. And these S curves have a long lifeline themselves. From the early 1960s, S-shaped curves were regularly employed for technological forecasting. Everett M. Rogers' diffusion of innovation theory (how innovations get accepted by the populace and spread) theorised that innovations would spread in society along an S curve. The idea has been applied since then across multiple domains. Fisher and Pry's studies of the substitution of new products for old in the 1970s showed that they broadly follow S-curve dynamics. S curves have since been applied to everything from the future of primary energy sources to the evolution of transportation systems, macro- and micro-economic trends, the growth of crime and terrorism, and environmental changes and associated challenges. Mann, in his work on systematic innovation for business, highlighted the use and application to even broader contexts. So, it is relatively safe to say, with perhaps fear of only a little contradiction, that S curves provide an accepted approach to how we think about most systems and their evolution.

Broadly, most systems have three phases on the S curve: early, middle and late. There are plenty of different versions of this cycle—some more detailed than others. But for our systems architect mindset, three phases are sufficient.

Phase 1: The Early Phase

During the early phase, the growth of performance of a system is slow compared to the effort, time and investment needed. This phase is often characterised by the development of a knowledge base around the new system. The basic knowledge required to ensure the system works fully is not yet understood. By the end of the early phase the knowledge base is developed, and improvements are beginning to increase rapidly. The S curve will slowly rise, and begin to rise faster as it moves into the middle period. Imagine you have implemented a totally new performance management system with an associated platform for the first time. At this early stage you will be building knowledge on what's working, what's not working, how people are using the system, how they are avoiding it. It is all about getting it to work—getting buy-in and gaining traction.

Phase 2: The Middle Phase

The middle phase is characterised by the growth of the systems performance as a deeper understanding of the knowledge base starts to yield many improvements at a lower level of investment. Adoption of the system is normally high at this stage, as the system becomes adapted in the organisation, and this ends up yielding increased potential investment spend. Imagine a new office design that has been implemented. Now that employees have been using it for a while, changes and improvements to layout can be made based on a greater understanding of how the space is being used day to day. Normally, around the halfway stage of the S curve, the rate of development or improvement will begin to slow. When the S curve begins to slow down, the system development will move into the late phase.

Phase 3: The Late Phase

The late phase is characterised by diminishing returns for every new investment made in the new system. Taking the performance management example, the system might now feel outdated due to a lack of significant new features being called for by the younger generations in the workforce. It is at the point where no more improvements can be made within the confines of the existing system and there needs to be a jump to the next one.

The Job System Example

Going deeper, let's think about the idea of 'the job' as a system (see Figure 4) that has evolved over time. Remember, if we are mapping a system and its evolution, it will have a lot of subsystems but for simplicity's sake, think about the overall system as 'the job'. Let's also realise that any S-curve plot must have a definition of what 'value' means for that system. So, let's go with 'meaning'—yes, a slightly esoteric idea, but good enough for our purposes (and something you will get a deeper understanding of as part of the societal whisperer mindset).

Back in the day (let's say the 1950's), it was enough to have a job—the level of meaning associated with that could only ever reach a certain plateau (the top of the S curve). You might be stuck in the same role, doing the same things repeatedly. Some more enlightened companies recognised the importance of creating more structured and interesting approaches to 'the job' and, as such, the idea of 'the career' was born, with a higher potential plateau of meaning associated. As we get closer to our current work state, companies now realise the idea of a much broader 'experience'[3]-led approach to work, with a focus on wellbeing, enabling higher levels of flexibility and perhaps greater empowerment through innovative forms of

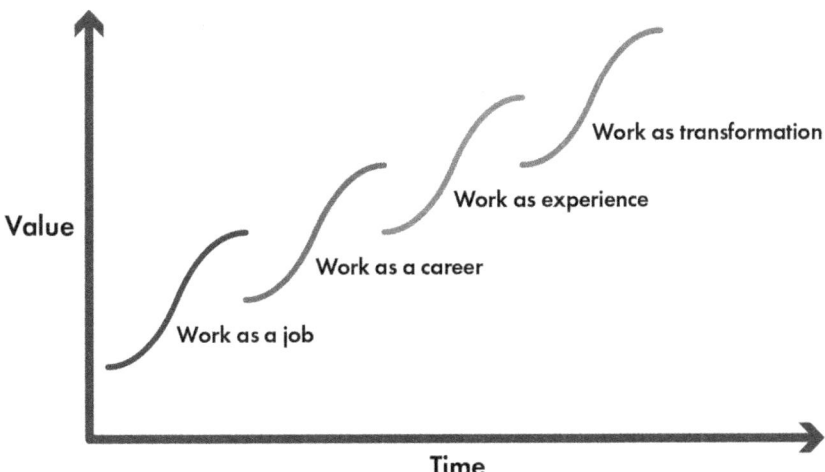

Figure 4   The job system

work design. This new system has enabled a new, higher plateau of meaning for the employee. It is not that the idea of 'the job' has died but a more evolved form (for the large part) will supersede it. As per the 'innovator's dilemma' (Christensen, 1997) and work conducted by various TRIZ researchers (Mann, 2002), new 'jumps' can at first feel like backward steps as the new system is just that—new—and it requires patience and improvement before it will fully supersede the previous system.

The Messy Hybrid Example

A slightly controversial example to highlight this is the S-curve plotting of place (of work) as the system and wellbeing as the value measure (see Figure 5). Again, an imperfect example but fine for illustration. Let's assume full 'Office' is the first system and 'Office + other place' (i.e., home) is seen as the next system (based on our research this is the next curve—over 70% of people are availing of hybrid work, with 83% highlighting it as a preferential way to work). From much research we can now see that regardless of how incredible an office setting is—one with all the perks and mod cons (!)—the drudge of getting to the office, with possibly a long commute, juggling life and work commitments, the constant interaction with various employees and the routineness of the office system, has a plateau when it

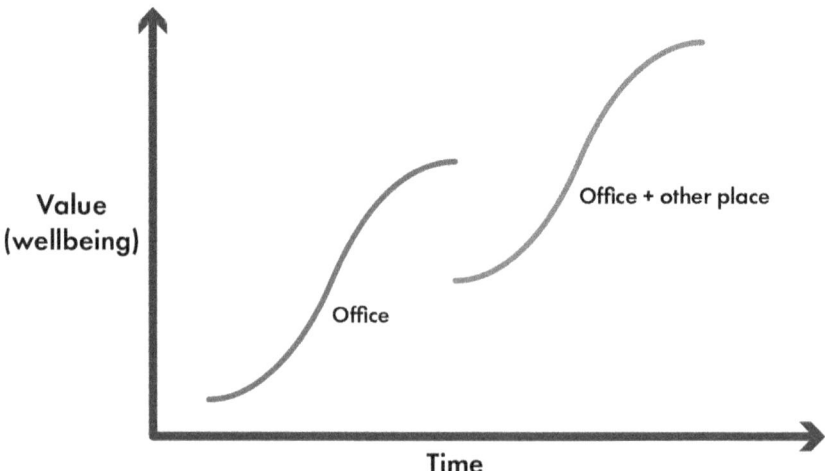

Figure 5   A hybrid example

comes to the wellbeing value dynamic. In advance of COVID, many organisations were already realising this and had started to implement place of work plus home working to improve overall wellbeing. But in the early days of this new type of working it was messy—new systems had to be introduced, leaders had to get comfortable with the lack of direct supervision and employees had to adapt to new ways of working. In fact, it still is messy in many organisations—especially in terms of leadership support. You will often find leaders who have lived predominantly through one curve experience harken back to that curve or that reality without fully understanding the potential higher-value plateaus provided by the new system.

UDS: Up, Down and Sideways

Thinking as a systems architect also means a realisation that there are often systems above the systems we are looking at, systems below it (subsystems) and even those subsystems may have subsystems. We may also have adjacent systems on either side of the system we are exploring. We may, in many instances, not have a complete system—we may have subsystems we are missing from our system!

By way of example, consider the 'package' system that you offer your employees. You may think of this system as having a few subsystems—pay, flexible working, benefits. But there are multiple adjacent systems (see Figure 6). From our work at the Future of Work Institute, we identified 20 subsystems that represent the entire proposition as an employer (commonly referred to an Employer Value Proposition). And each of these subsystems will be at different stages of evolution in an organisation, and each will have different levels of importance dependent on the cohorts, generations or groupings within a business. On one engagement with a particular organisation in a tech subsector, we uncovered the importance placed by younger employees on the level of technology made available to them as part of their role. This subsystem became an important, and relatively inexpensive, retention mechanism for that organisation's total proposition. So, in this case we have one core supersystem—Proposition; multiple subsystems—Proposition elements; and these will also have their own subsystems. For example, the 'Benefits and Perks' subsystem will also comprise lower-level subsystems.

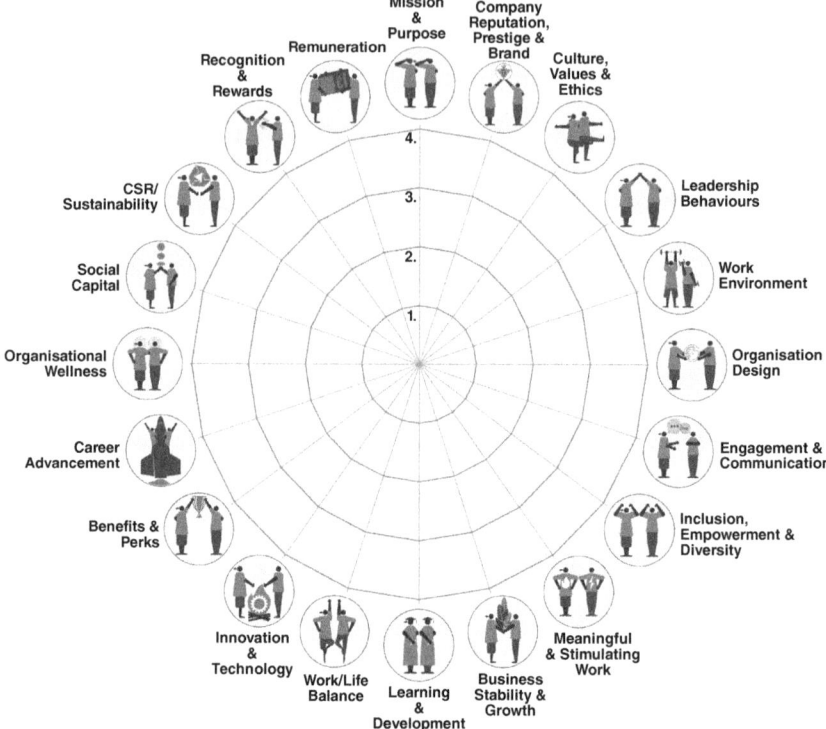

Figure 6   FOWI employer value proposition 'system'

Everywhere along these 'up', 'down' and 'sideways' systems there are opportunities to evolve, improve and innovate. As systems architects, we need to make sure we are always asking:

- Have we captured the full system?
- Are there systems on top of the systems that we are looking at?
- What are the systems below?
- What are the systems either side?
- Are we missing systems?

Only by consciously asking these types of questions consistently can we unlock the true power of systems thinking.

The Ideality Equation

When it comes to the systems architect mindset, no concept is more powerful, more perpetually useful, than that of ideality. Ideality is one of the key principles of TRIZ, a methodology developed by Genrikh Altshuller, a patent clerk in Russia, in the 1940s. Ideality represents the goal or solution to a problem where the system delivers maximum benefits (all the benefits) with minimal or no cost, complexity or harmful effects (none of the harm).

In a way, all systems are evolving to better, more ideal forms. Any platform you work on, any online interface you have used is evolving towards some form of ideality. The specific nature of that ideality will differ depending on context. Amazon 1-Click? An example of ideality in action—one click versus multiple clicks. Numerous HR and people platforms are built on some variation of promises that centre around 'zero', 'less', 'more', 'fully', 'all'—less time, less energy, more output, more productivity, fully personalised.

We can apply the ideality concept to anything. Here are a few examples:

- The Ideal Final Product is a product that delivers all the desired functions of the product—more specifically, the main useful functions and other desirable functions.
- The Ideal Process is a process that gives all the desired outcomes of the process without involving any time, effort, energy or resources.
- The Ideal Technique is a technique that requires nothing expensive, involves nothing difficult and achieves all the results.
- The Ideal Office is one that give you all the benefits of an office without the overheads, fixtures and fittings, and depreciation.

You get the idea. I sum it all up by calling it 'backward thinking'. Instead of thinking about the system as where it is now, think about the ideal system—whatever system you are looking at—and work backwards. Think about what all the benefits would look like, and what removing all the harm and costs would look like. From this you will get a sense of what things are in flow with ideality and what are not.

In relation to research, for example, my 'ideal' statement might be: I want all the research I need, in the format I need it, with practically zero effort or zero time spent on gathering the information. For the more astute amongst you (ChatGPT anyone?), according to Altshuller, from his book *And Suddenly the Inventor Appeared*: '(Ideality)[4] is a fantasy, a dream. It cannot be reached, but it will allow us to build a path to the solution. . . .' But in the age of AI are many of these ideals, once fantasies and dreams, now possible realities? You will see more on ideality in Part II of the book. For now, just think backwards to go forwards!

Bottom Line

You now have a comprehensive system definition for the future of work. This includes 3 Ws and 16 equalisers. Everything in your future work world is a system, and those systems evolve over time based on key value aspects. Every system has subsystems, and even those subsystems have subsystems. As system architects we always need to be looking up, down and sideways to get a full view of all the systems that we can improve and innovate. Thinking in 'ideality' gives a true north compass that will help you go forwards by thinking backwards.

Practically, reflect on a system you are working on. Understand its subsystems and their evolution as curves. Attempt to plot their relative maturity against the most important value criteria elements you can think off. Define their ideal state and work backwards. Congratulations! You are now thinking like a systems architect—you will be surprised how it helps you to see with greater clarity and uncovers new avenues for exploration.

Jump 2: Immersive Induction

Extract from article 'It's not try before you buy but feel before you fix'. The full article by Rogers Nelson in *The Next of Times* (April 23, 2030) highlights the increasing use of immersive practices by organisations to continuously entice and excite potential candidates in an age of severe talent competition.

Organisations are working harder than ever to entice potential candidates. Utilising the latest in immersive augmented and virtual realities—and a natural evolution of organisations becoming more accessible—'immersive induction' enables potential future employees—from school-goers to experienced professionals— to gain real-world insights on working within their targeted and preferred places to work.

At Energy Pulse, one of the largest sustainable energy companies in Europe, potential candidates can go on a VR maintenance callout with an Energy Pulse employee and get a sense of a day in the life of the maintenance technician. People Experience Director Shayz Vaze says: 'This approach is really working. Last month more than 105 of our preferred candidates submitted CVs and more than 27 apprentices have been hired this quarter alone. The VR journey really takes away what I call the "After Shock" of joining the business. One of the surprising outcomes of immersive induction at Energy Pulse is that some employees have become minor social celebrities—Fabian Deyer, a middle-aged technician and father of two, has become a bit of a hit due to the laconic and often "flowery" language he uses on his callouts!'

At one of the most innovative architectural firms in Singapore—SXI—they have created an architectural playground platform that enables third- and fourth-year university students to input into live architectural projects and in a small way experience the real world of the practicing architect. One unexpected outcome of this initiative has been the exponential increase in the diversity of their global candidate poll. According to partner Jess Blade: 'It's unbelievable—we are getting participation from over 200 universities, and this is leading to all sorts of diverse inputs and inspirations. We intend to create a "chaos group" of students from different continents all over the world to compete to "break architecture"—should be fun!'

It might be a little early to tell if this trend is more fundamental than fad, but it has become a lot easier to develop these types of experiences with no code platforms and headsets that have become ubiquitous due to falling costs. What it is fair to say is we are living in an age where induction is no longer something that happens when you join an organisation. It is an always-on strategy focused on continuously engaging prospective or targeted candidates with experiences that enable them to really feel what it's like to fix their sights on their next work destination.

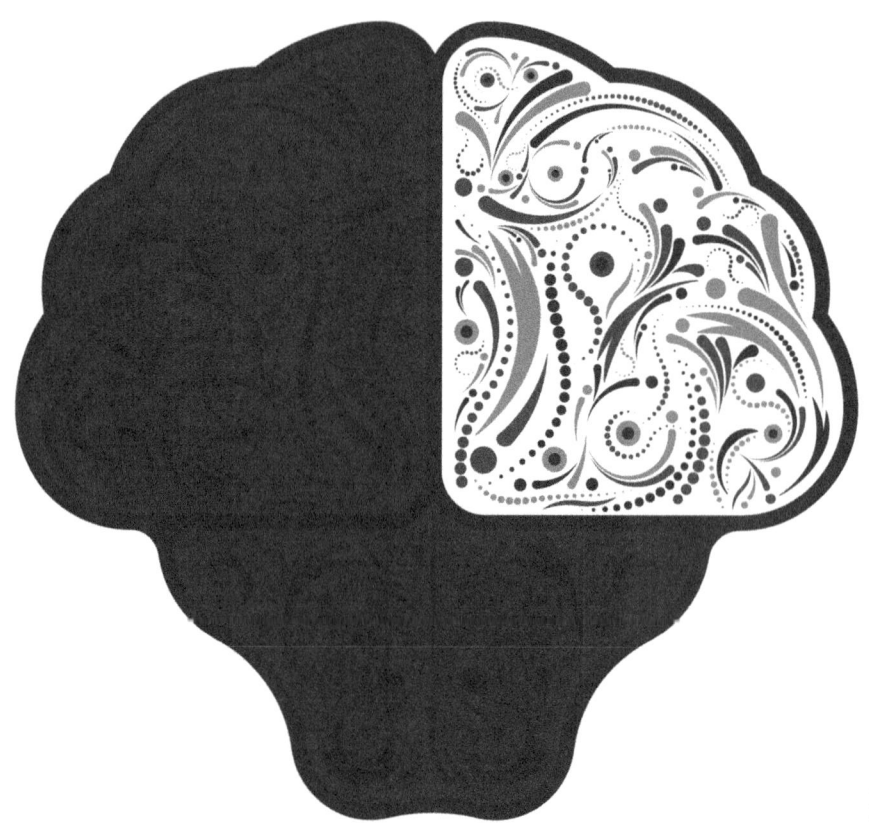

2

Mindset Two: The Societal Whisperer

Yearnings. If I was to sum up much of the commentary about the future of work and of organisations, it is captured in that one word. Strong yearnings for organisations that are human, highly ethical, living and breathing organisms. Equally deep yearnings for organisations that are hyper-efficient, autonomous machines doing all sorts of incredible things by themselves. Other yearnings for fully circular organisations that will save us from environmental calamity.

But what is the 'why' behind these yearnings? How do we understand what drives our societal thinking? Why, for example, do we see calls for four-day weeks? For universal wages? For leaders to become more like healers? For organisations to be more 'regenerative'? For experiences and transformations? Manifestos to re-wild and re-invent ourselves and our work, calls for the ethical use of exponential technologies? Why is it that some countries pursue what we might perceive as less enlightened workplace policies than others? Why will certain approaches work in one context and not in another? I asked these and plenty of other questions many moons ago across many projects. And these questions lead us nicely to our second mindset, the societal whisperer, and to the most useful developmental model I have ever used.

This mindset is about truly seeing the underlying layers of societal evolution and human consciousness. Sounds like a big concept? It is. This mindset is based primarily on a deep methodology known as 'spiral dynamics' and my own experiences of utilising it in organisational contexts. Some have heard of spiral dynamics; many have not. In my experience, its power is rarely utilised and its application is not commonplace. Originally introduced by Professor Clare W. Graves (Graves, 1970), it is a psychological and development model which proposes that societal progress has evolved in a series of stages with a distinct world view. It has been called—to paraphrase others—the underlying DNA of society. The original work has been further developed by Beck and Cowan (1996) to apply it to business contexts and societal change. There are a couple of great books on the topic that apply these ideas more deeply in organisational settings: *Teal Dots in an Orange World* (Østergaard, 2019) and the original book that brought spiral dynamics specifically to organisation design: *Reinventing Organizations* (Laloux, 2014). Both are great references to delve deeper into some of the concepts discussed here and I'd recommend both.[1]

In the foreword to *Spiral Dynamics in Action* (Beck et al., 2018), Ronnie Lessem highlights how spiral dynamics is 'arguably the first, major, systemic and conceptual system that addresses the big picture'. To put it simply, and in my own words, spiral dynamics enables us to see the world in a much more strategic and holistic way. And as such it is a key aspect to how we think about the now and next of work. The experts in this field would argue that spiral dynamics is the overreaching concept across all these mindsets—which is not wrong. However, from our experience of using these concepts in an organisational and applied context, it needs to be integrated with the other mindsets to be practically useful.

The Model

At its core, spiral dynamics suggests that human consciousness develops in a spiral, moving through levels or stages of increasing complexity and differentiation. The model is rooted in the idea that human beings and societies respond to the challenges they face by adopting new ways of thinking, being and doing.

The stages are not hierarchical but represent a dynamic, emergent process (hence the use of a three-dimensional spiral to highlight this process). Each new stage is a response to the limitations or deficiencies of the previous one, creating a continuous cycle of growth and transformation.

The stages are equally applicable at a national level, as well as at an organisational and individual level. For example, Denmark could be seen as predominantly a green-code society with elements of yellow; China predominantly red/orange; the United States predominantly orange. It is no accident, for example, that some of the first design thinking programmes originated in Denmark (like Utopia).

The Stages of Spiral Dynamics: The Codes

The stages in spiral dynamics are mostly represented by colours (see Figure 7). Each colour, known as a code, corresponds to a specific worldview or value system that shapes how people see and interact with the

Figure 7 The colours and pictures associated with the codes

world. These stages are summarised very simply (see the Appendix[2] for more detailed information on each code) as follows:

1. **Beige (Survivalistic)**
   - The Beige level represents the basic survival stage, where the primary concern is meeting fundamental needs like food, water and shelter. This stage is seen in infants, primitive societies or situations of extreme survival.
   - Key Value: Basic survival instincts and automatic responses.
   - Worldview: 'Survive'.
2. **Purple (Tribalistic)**
   - The Purple level is centred around tribalism, magic and ritual. People in this stage focus on group identity and allegiance, with an emphasis on tradition, safety and the preservation of the tribe's customs.
   - Key Value: Safety through belonging to a tribe or group.
   - Worldview: 'Follow the rules of tradition'.
3. **Red (Egocentric)**
   - The Red level is characterised by power and impulsive behaviour. People at this stage seek to assert their dominance and individuality. The worldview is driven by ego, with an emphasis on achieving personal power and status.
   - Key Value: Power and control.
   - Worldview: 'I will dominate'.
4. **Blue (Absolutistic)**
   - The Blue level is marked by a belief in absolute truths, laws and moral codes. Individuals and societies at this stage are guided by order, discipline and the pursuit of stability. Blue is associated with religious and legal systems that offer certainty and structure.
   - Key Value: Order, discipline and certainty.
   - Worldview: 'There is one truth, and it must be followed'.
5. **Orange (Achievistic)**
   - The Orange level is associated with scientific thinking, individual achievement and progress. People at this stage value material success,

rationality and autonomy. They seek to master the world through innovation, entrepreneurship and the pursuit of knowledge.

- Key Value: Achievement and success through individual effort.
- Worldview: 'Let's get things done rationally'.

6. Green (Humanistic)
   - The Green level emphasises equality, empathy and community. It is driven by a desire for social justice, environmental sustainability and inclusivity. People in this stage prioritise relationships, cooperation and understanding diverse perspectives.
   - Key Value: Compassion, equality and social harmony.
   - Worldview: 'We are all in this together'.

7. Yellow (Integrative)
   - The Yellow level represents a more integrative, systemic worldview. It focuses on flexibility, complexity and seeing the interconnectedness of all things. People at this stage can embrace paradoxes and integrate knowledge from multiple perspectives to solve problems.
   - Key Value: Integrating complexity and seeing the whole system.
   - Worldview: 'We are part of a larger system'.

8. Turquoise (Holistic)
   - The Turquoise level represents a highly integrated, global and spiritual perspective. People at this stage operate with a deep sense of collective purpose, understanding the interconnectedness of all life and working towards global harmony.
   - Key Value: Collective wellbeing and spiritual interconnectedness.
   - Worldview: 'We are all part of a unified whole'.

One Code, Many Codes

A key point is that even when there is an evolution to another code, that code includes every other code that came before it. The analogy often used to explain this is the 'tree-ring analogy', where the outer ring is the newest but it is an outcome of all the other tree rings that have come before it and can't exist without it. It is also important to note that no level is inherently 'bad' or 'good'—all have their respective strengths and weaknesses. And we can often see healthy and unhealthy expressions of the same predominant system.

According to Ghorashi (2014), author of *Memenomics: The Next-Generation Economic System*, each level or value system can exhibit both healthy and unhealthy aspects (often called expressions). A good example provided by Ghorashi is Google's business practices representing a healthy expression of the orange code system, whilst Wall Street's practices might appear as an unhealthy expression of the same orange code system. Neither code is inherently good or bad. Every code has good aspects and bad aspects associated with it.

The Leap

The codes are split into two categories: the first six are known as the first-tier or subsistence codes; the last two (second-tier codes) are a glimpse into the near future. It is generally agreed that these codes came into existence about 50 years ago. Many authors in this space write about the 'leap' into the second-tier codes and will it happen or not. In some of the research, Scandinavian countries like Denmark are seen as societies that could make the leap fully into second-tier consciousness, given that they are predominantly green code. It can be difficult to get your head around some of the future ideas—to many of us, they may seem fluffy or 'out there'—in many ways, much of the 'why' behind the calls for regeneration, rewilding and so on comes from the aspiration to jump to the second tier of thinking and doing. The challenge is that much of the world, and the organisations that inhabit it, are still predominantly blue and orange, and the 'jump' will mean significant reconsideration of what society is and indeed what the new purpose of organisations actually is.

The DNA of Business

So, how can we use these ideas to think about the future of work in practice? If you can imagine a DNA code based on spiral dynamics that represents most organisations (see Figure 8), it probably looked like the left image of Figure 8 for the past fifty years. Broadly, most organisations have had a deep and unwavering focus on market competitiveness and the creation of shareholder value (orange), coupled with an order, compliance and process hierarchy.

For anyone who remembers the impassioned Michael Douglas speech from *Wall Street*, with the core idea that 'greed is good', it possibly sums up the modern era of business. The genetic code of most organisations in the

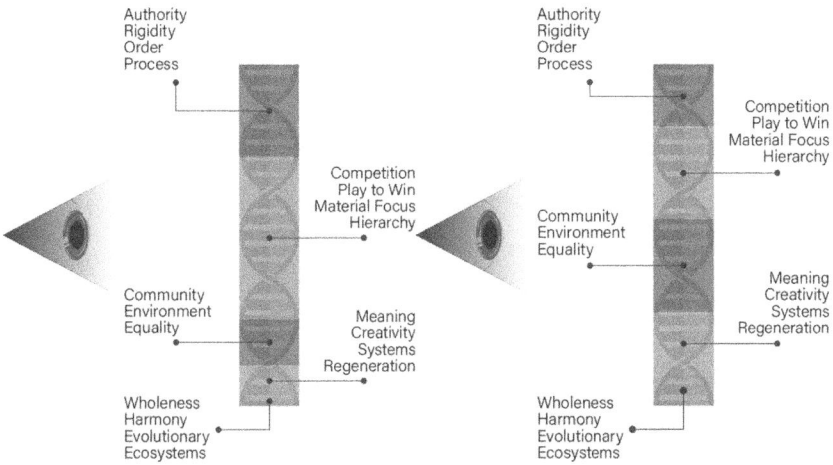

Figure 8 The evolving DNA of organisations

modern era would have looked predominantly orange and blue, with very little of anything else. A lot of good stuff and bad stuff has come from that era. As with all eras, there are often outliers, islands of future work, sprinklings of more 'next code' thinking—like Cadbury and its (at the time) unprecedented care for its workers; co-operatives like Mondragon with a deep, empowering focus on member ownership; and Patagonia, an early innovator in sustainability and net positive impact.

In this current era we can see a broad evolution of this DNA. There's a growth of green thinking (mostly enforced due to environmental calamity and associated new regulatory practices), with small sprinklings of yellow and teal in some organisations. We could view these changes as a direct response to the 'bad' aspects of red, blue and orange practices. For example, data suggests that today there are over 10 million social enterprises (predominantly green) that authentically put purpose before profit, tackling pressing issues like climate change and poverty. The social enterprise sector is now bigger than the telecom and apparel industries in terms of annual revenue.

There is a growth in organisations like B Corp, focused on promoting enlightened and purpose-driven practices. Concepts like regenerative business, continuous learning and a drive to bring 'the whole self' to work are all examples of yellow and teal thinking that are also gaining some traction. How widespread in actual practice are these concepts? I'm not convinced. Talking 'green', 'yellow' and 'teal' doesn't mean organisations are green, yellow and teal. In many cases it represents an aspiration driven by future-age-thinking authors and commentators but in reality, the organisation's natural default is still very much orange. Pragmatists—and I would consider myself one—consider much more of an 'and' approach as a meaningful path forward. How can we be a better orange and have more of a green focus. The WEF (World Economic Forum), holding a pragmatic stance themselves, have been calling for a 'new capitalism'—an approach that proposes a continued focus on 'better' organisation and shareholder (good orange) value coupled with more purpose-driven, net beneficial practices (green). The previously mentioned book by Østergaard also takes this practical approach, suggesting that the more evolved codes can find a place in more traditional organisations and provide excellent examples on the same.

Practical Principles on How to Use the Societal Whisperer Mindset

You have probably realised at this point that there is huge depth to a lot of these concepts. This one chapter, just a small slice, can only give you a start on your societal mindset journey but here are some practical principles that should help you along the way that I have learned through real-world application. Remember to refer to the Appendix at the back of the book for a deeper dive into the codes.

1. **All the 'colours' exist in an organisation, in business units and teams, but certain colours will predominate—watch out for them.**

   We have worked with organisations that are predominantly orange but have one business unit that is mostly green. You will often find pockets of 'next codes' sprinkled throughout your organisation. By way of example, my business unit—the Future of Work Institute (FOWI)—is predominantly green/yellow: deep collaboration, a focus on enabling people to transform through self-created project development and a leadership model based on the idea of a collective 'band'. This is different to the broader business, which would be more 'good' orange/green (due to context and the sector it is in), with a growing focus on sustainable practices but a predominant focus on direct commercial success.

2. **Change or improvement is often about moving towards a more predominant code, or making a code a 'bit more something'.**

    As part of any change or improvement initiative, think about what underlying DNA you are trying to create or move towards. This will help you to understand the magnitude of change required. For example, you might be trying to create a more green/yellow code within your business unit, but are starting from a deep blue/orange focus. In this instance it might make sense to conduct a few selected key spotlight initiatives that are more green code in nature (with a focus on deep collaboration, for example) as a stepping stone to the new code. In FOWI projects I will often use 'code plus thinking', focused on the addition of two codes applied to key questions:

    - How can we have control (blue) **and** give greater empowerment (green)?
    - How can we be hyper-efficient (orange) **and** deeply human (yellow)?
    - How can we be capitalist (orange) **and** socialist (yellow)?
    - How can we be about profit (orange) **and** purpose (green)?
    - How can we train (orange) **and** authentically transform (teal) our people?
    - How can we think about the next-year impact of what we do (orange) **and** the next 100 years (teal)?

3. Adding time and condition elements helps to really make the ideas above practical and actionable. For example, in relation to the first statement above, we can ask: When do we need to have more team control and when can we have greater team empowerment? Under what conditions might we allow greater levels of empowerment? At what stages of projects or processes do we need greater levels of control and at what stages can we be more freeform? The next or preceding code can look a bit mad, but the idea is to use a means to explore what that code might mean, or even what parts of the code might mean.

If you go deep on the yellow and teal (second-tier) codes, some of the ideas may feel strange, out there, alien. This is normal as they represent a genuine societal shift. The same challenges can apply if you are a highly blue or orange code and you look at some of the principles of the green code. The important thing to recognise is that the next codes provide avenues for thinking, creativity and evolution and they are worth exploring. What is equally important to bear in mind is that we may also look to adopting a preceding code. For example, if an organisation is struggling in the marketplace, then a short-term 'red code' approach—utilising the best elements of red code thinking—might very well be the most appropriate strategy for success. The important aspect is to play to the positive aspects of that code rather than the negative for balanced transformation.

4. **The codes can be used to re-design or re-think existing practices by looking through the different codes—it's not about doing things but doing things through the code.**

   Probably the most useful way to utilise the codes in the real world is to look at initiatives and ask questions like 'What if this was a teal initiative, what would it look like?'. So, for example, and in reference to a previous FOWI client project, if you have a wellness initiative, how 'whole' or holistic is it? How does it integrate the whole human? Is it too narrow in its focus? Will it create a level of not just performance (orange) and connection (green) but will it also enable some level of transformation of the individual (teal)? If you have a leadership programme, are you tapping into green and yellow codes? For example, Lego's 'Leadership Playground'[3] approach to foster leadership development emphasises a safe and inclusive space for exploration and learning and is rooted in the way children play and interact in a playground setting. It encourages behaviours like bravery, curiosity and focus—very much yellow code in nature.

5. **There are lots of examples out there of these codes in practice, and it's not always where you think.**

   Once you start seeing through colours it drives you to find examples of practice across multiple areas. It even helps you to 'catalogue' and classify knowledge. For example, *Leader as Healer* (Janni, 2023) is a superb book and very much represents yellow/teal code principles. But you will also be drawn to unexpected islands like the GAA (Ireland's Gaelic Athletics Association), an amateur organisation with a deep green and yellow DNA. You will recognise many co-operative movements as deeply teal. And most importantly it will open you up to unexpected sources and design inputs for your own future work world.

Bottom Line

As a societal whisper, we understand that there are underlying social patterns that can help explain all sorts of interesting societal and organisational developments. Spiral dynamics and its associated codes can be a powerful approach to look at things in deeper ways, explain likely evolutions in response to change and act as a powerful social architecture.

Practically, reflect on an initiative you are working on. Challenge yourself to think about what code you are designing it through. Have you thought about tapping into some of the principles and ideas from other codes? How might it make you think differently about that initiative? In what unexpected areas might you find ideas for new codes that you could apply? Congratulations! You are now thinking a little more like a societal whisperer—you will be surprised how it helps you to create initiatives that more naturally connect.

Jump 3: TFI

Introduction to the brochure for 'The Integral Company: Your next collaborative advantage'.

First flown in 2031, The Flag Integral (TFI) was developed by a consortium of forward-thinking organisations along with a new ISO standard for inclusiveness and integration. It was created in the wake of significant backlash to diversity, equity and inclusion (DE&I) initiatives across some countries in Europe and the Americas in the mid-2020s. The primary purpose of the flag is to have a highly visible symbol that highlights how DE&I has moved beyond initiatives and into full integration across strategic and operational business practices. Enough meaningful case studies of performance success have been generated by the 100 companies involved, showcasing the validity of this 'new way'. The impact has been likened to that of the six sigma and lean movements, which originated in the 1970s and 1980s and became watch words for operational efficiency.

Only the most inclusive and integrated organisations can fly the flag. Evidence must be provided to show the diverse and inclusive practices are fully embedded across activities such as:

- *Attraction & Employer Marketing*
- *Recruitment & Onboarding*
- *Project Team Selection & Project Delivery*
- *Leadership Development & Practices*
- *New Process, Service and Product Innovation*
- *Employee Experience & Engagement*
- *Supplier Selection & Partnerships*
- *Technology Development & Ethical AI*

There also must be a clear and evidence-based approach to the impact of integrating these practices across key performance indicators in the business.

The flag design, created by famed design house A-LD, represents how multiple colours—representative of diversity in all its forms—when properly harnessed, lead to the transformational white light of continuous change, empowerment, enlightenment and business energy.

3

Mindset Three: The Destination Designer

When I was a kid, my favourite destination was the theatre or, to be more precise, the musical theatre. I can still remember the musty, earthy smell of those red, frayed theatre seats, as I sat there as a very good boy (!) waiting for my mother to complete her run throughs. She was a musical director, and I would be amazed at how a show would come together over weeks and months and turn into something magical. Something that was more than the sum of its parts and something with a serious attention to detail. As I got a little older, I realised the gap between amateur musical productions and professional ones. The big differences in the level of production, direction and storytelling. For any of you who have been at another globally recognised destination—Disneyland—the differences between that and a general amusement park—the predecessor to Disneyland—are stark. Or if you aren't a Disney fan, think Efteling (for those of you lucky enough to have visited that magical Dutch fairytale park). And it's not due to money. It's due to attention to detail. It's about how that overall experience is designed, delivered and consistently reinforced to create meaning, magic and momentum.

What has all of this got to do with the mindsets needed for your future work world I hear you say? The fact is, whether you like it or not, your organisations are destinations—destinations for talent—and that destination may very well not live up to the destinations you had in your head a moment ago. They might be more 'meh' than magic; more mediocre than marvellous. Any organisation, just like any good destination, must be purposefully and professionally designed. And everyone has a design role in making it happen. The CEO is responsible for the now and next design of their organisation's future work world. The CPO/CHRO is responsible for co-designing the experience of the employees throughout their entire career journey. The team lead is responsible for designing not just the experience of the team but also how the work gets delivered. And yet a design mindset is a mindset that few fully adopt. In fact, it is unlikely that most of the people (or roles, to be more precise) just mentioned would see themselves as designers. As a result, key initiatives are often designed with limited involvement of the users who are going to be impacted by the initiative. Poor design—or lack of any design—at strategic and operational levels is often at the core of many of the failed projects that litter most organisations.

So, our second key mindset is the Destination Designer mindset. At its core, this mindset is about a recognition that we must purposefully design organisations and fully harness a design-centred approach.

Poorly Designed Destinations

Now, to be slightly controversial for a moment, I don't believe in general terms that many organisations are true destinations for talent—one that people will make a special effort to be part of or one that is worthy of an extended stay.

For all the workplace awards and the growing prevalence of an awards culture across many sectors, the latest research from the Future of Work Institute (FOWI, 2024–2025) highlights that many people are still leaving organisations due to what I would see as poor design, including:

- Poor leadership 35–42%
- Lack of recognition 32%
- Company culture 25–30%
- Toxic work environment 27%
- Poor colleague relationships 20–25%

- Exit interviews 50–55%
- Feedback 30–35%
- Consider lev 80–83%

Using our destination designer's mindset, we would view all the challenges above as opportunities to design or re-design. To think perhaps differently about things and explore new avenues for improvement. Reflect for a moment on one or some of your best employees and think about how they might answer the following questions (or indeed how you would answer them) about your organisation. Imagine for a moment they are speaking with friends, not filling out a questionnaire. The questions are derived and adapted from applied research on authentic place association (D'Orey et al., 2019), which focuses on belonging, commitment, affection and identification—powerful pillars that make a place memorable and transformative.

Belonging to a Place

The events that occur during my time here are important to me.
My experiences in this place had a big effect on me.

Commitment to a Place

I would leave my country or city and go to work in this place.
I recognise myself in the lifestyle of the people who work in this place.
I'm ready to invest my time and talent to improve this place.
This place has a lot to do with me.

Affection for a Place

It would be a very good place to come back to even after I have left
  for a while.
I love this place and, if I could, I would spend more time in it.

Identification with a Place

To me, interviewing to join this place wasn't strange.
I'm ready to dedicate myself body and soul to preserving the values of
  this place.
After being in this place, I feel that it's part of me.

In a way, these questions really raise the bar about how truly our best (and indeed worst) employees associate with our 'place'. They also get us thinking like true destination designers—focusing on both the rational and the emotional human aspects of work, getting to the core of it all and understanding that we need to go deep as designers to uncover design opportunities to make things better for our human 'users'.

Design—Nothing New

Now design is nothing new. And the power of design and design thinking has been extolled and innovated by organisations like IDEO, the Design Council and many more over the years. It also has its critics (I'm not doing a deep dive on this—check the references in the Bibliography for some of the debate). But at this stage even the most cynical of commentators (given the plethora of successful case examples out there) would highlight that using a design-based approach has its merits. There are also multiple off-shoots and interrelated branches of design: human-centred design, inclusive design, interface design, services design, experience design and more. It can get, frankly, a little confusing. But let us not worry about the size of the design wave. Let us worry about the motion of the design ocean. There are some key principles we use consistently at the FOWI that are powerful when it comes to the mindset we need for exploring and designing our future work worlds. A bit of a mishmash of principles, mostly extracted from experience, place and thinking design fields.

Human Centricity

'Nothing for us without us'[1] smartly surmises the essence of this principle. By most standards, any design process worth its salt involves people, or users, and puts them right at the centre. And this means really at the centre. It means observing how someone is doing something in context; it means enabling people to play and engage with prototypes or options and understanding their experiences. It also means moving beyond what people are thinking into how they feel, and the various emotions associated with that. Think, for example, about the last global talent attraction campaign you ran. Did you really get behind the psychology of the group or cohort you were trying to attract? Did you use people in the cohort to help you design, test and adjust the campaign? That last benefit programme you created—was it designed with the employees' life stages in mind, or was it one size fits all? What parts of it are important to them? What emotions were you attempting to elicit from your audience at your last town hall jamboree and did you know enough about them to really design for that emotion? Once we start realising the power of true human centricity, we will start to see flaws in our designs all over the place—and that is a good thing. As a leader myself I have a saying I use often with my FOWI team: 'inclusive fear leads to inherent failure'. By this I mean that if you don't get involvement early on from the humans you are creating for, for whatever reason, then you have already built future failure into your design.

Diverge–Converge

Diverge–converge really is the pumping heart of the design mindset. There are many versions of it, and some have one 'diamond' (as it's called) or a 'double diamond', but fundamentally it comes down to a few key steps that I like to call 'What Really Is, What Could Be, What Will Be'. The actual visual of the diverge–converge looks like a diamond on its side (see Figure 9). All the projects at the FOWI use the process. But a process is just a process without the experience of using it. Here is what we've learned to help you think, at least a little more, like a destination designer.

Stage One: What Really Is

This stage focuses on understanding what really is going on in the particular area, scope, challenge or opportunity that you are applying design thinking to. This phase is often called the discovery phase—I like to call it the 'uncover phase' as it is often the phase where we uncover different views or perspectives on long-held beliefs.

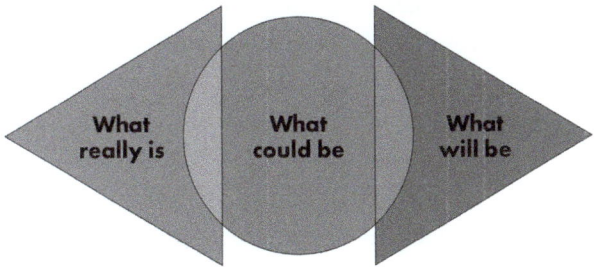

Figure 9   Simplified design process

Our practical experience is that this stage is primarily about two things: questions/discussions and immersions.

Questions: At this stage the big question is 'why?' Why is something the way it is, why do we do it like that, why do people think that, why is a particular process designed the way it is, why is a new trend worth considering for us? At the FOWI we use the principle of Shoshin to keep us open and honest at this uncover phase. A Japanese Zen term, Shoshin translates as 'beginner's mind' and relates to a fundamental contradiction: the more you know about a subject, the more likely you are to close your mind to new learnings or fresh perspectives. In his book *Zen Mind, Beginner's Mind* (1970), Zen monk Shunryu Suzuki highlights that 'In the beginner's mind there are many possibilities, but in the expert's, there are few'. Thomas Kuhn discovered that most paradigm shifts in science are brought about either by young people or by people who were originally trained in a different discipline. This happens because these people are not biased towards the Einstellung effect, a negative effect of previous experience when solving new problems. In essence, Shoshin is about adopting an open mind—one of curiosity and understanding. There will always be an abundance of so-called experts on a topic that you must harness but not allow to overtake a process of curiosity.

For example, when we work with organisations mapping their 'As Is (Really Is)' future work worlds, often HR teams will rate their 'As Is' on a particular area (or equalisers, which you will learn more about in Part III) higher than non-HR people in the room. That team will have worked extremely hard to create a people or talent initiative that, from their perspective, is almost perfect. I worked with an organisation that had a relatively comprehensive organisational wellness programme but very few employees utilised it or engaged with it. During the uncover phase, where we simply asked, 'Why aren't people using the programme?', it became apparent that the HR team didn't fully involve the people they were designing the programme for in any meaningful way, and many didn't understand what the programme was or how it would really benefit them personally. The important thing here is to be curious and open as to why things are a certain way and see it as an opportunity for exploration, innovation and possible re-invention.

I like to use the comfortable/uncomfortable philosophy to sense check how deep we are going—if we are too comfortable with the process at this stage and we are getting easy answers, we aren't asking the right questions. We need to get to a level of discomfort to really know that the process is right.

The following is a list of good questions/prompts that I often use to break into a real view. Note the use of emotive language: tone up or down based on your cultural/personal norms (and in no way use anything offensive), but make sure to use emotive language—our experience tells us that it gets you to a more honest place.

- *Why is this process crap?*
- *Ten things I/we hate about the experience.*
- *Why do I/we think this approach is perfect?*
- *Why did I/we design it this way?*
- *Five reasons we should do nothing.*
- *Why is this strategy killing us/me?*
- *Why would we/I speak about this at an awards ceremony?*
- *Why are the questions we are asking right or wrong?*
- *Three pieces of evidence that support my/our position.*
- *Why does this make me/us look like (an) amateur(s) in a world of professionals?*

Immersions: If questions represent the verbal of the 'What Really Is' phase, then immersions represent the tactile. Standing back to watch how a group interacts, observing a process in action or how a strategy or initiative is actually happening in the real world gives a different dimension to the 'Really Is' phase. There are loads of ways to do this and, if I were you, I would tap into some of the amazing work being done in areas like organisation anthropology to get great insights. A good colleague of mine, from a psychology background, will often just spend time sitting in a canteen to immerse themselves in the culture and atmosphere of a place. You get the idea!

Stage Two: What Could Be

This stage is about stretching thinking as best you can around the area you have focused on. Many of us tend to go from questions to solutions in a fairly straight line, as opposed to really swishing around in the 'what ifs'. We have a simple rule for this phase—call it the Winkless Law if you like (ego trip): 'if it doesn't feel crazy at this stage you probably aren't being crazy enough' with your ideas and concepts. What you are coming up with should make you extremely uncomfortable and very stupid, at least in some instances. From the hundreds of sessions we have facilitated there seems to be a general truth that you will get a 1:10:3 ratio—one mad idea, ten criticisms or moans, and a drive for about three actions. When you get to the Model part of this book you will be able to play with the 16 continuums to help you stretch thinking but for the purposes of our broader destination designer mindset, let me introduce a powerful set of statements to help you tap into all sorts of crazy goodness. (The astute amongst you will see the link to ideality from the systems architect mindset.) Use them with the age old 'what if':

- All of X
- Nothing of X
- A different X

For example, we might be exploring our workplace: What if we had no offices? What if we had all of the locations for all of our employees? What if we did something different to an office? What if we had all of the implicit wisdom, none of the wisdom waste when employees leave? What if we had a different approach or a unique way to capture wisdom? You get the idea. Give it a go!

Stage 3: What Will Be

This stage is all about getting back from the 'Could Be' stage and moving into action. Action from a designer's perspective can often mean the creation of some experiments to test. In a way, experimenting could be seen as another key principle of the designer's mindset, given its importance. How many times have you been part of a change programme, or an initiative that didn't hit the spot? This is often due to a lack of experimentation to really test, learn and then adjust elements accordingly. A key concept here is 'Lo Fi is better than No Fi' meaning that a very unsophisticated, low-cost test is better than no test at all. For example, on a project I participated in, an organisation in the professional services space was rolling out a completely new sales/service organisation structure. With a view that it would bring all sorts of benefits. Lots of best practices and very fancy diagrams abounded. And of course, a lot of expensive tech. They were all going in big from day one. It became apparent that only a small group had been involved in its design. No testing was going to be done. I suggested a one-day 'real-world' test, using a one-team mix of frontline sales and service employees, working in this (at the time) hypothetical structure and set of new processes with a fictional set of customers. Within about four hours major flaws became apparent with the approach and by the end of the day new modified approaches were suggested that might make the whole thing work. That one-day, Lo Fi experiment really saved another re-design destined for the organisational rubbish heap. So, ask yourself, what do we need to learn? What should we test? What can we pilot? Go Shoshin even at this phase.

DBR: Depth, Breadth and Richness

This principle I have learned the hard way over the years, and it really refers to the fact that a destination designer has a huge depth, breadth and richness available—if they so choose to tap into it. Let me explain. If we are designing a new office space (it could equally be a new onboarding process, or a new engagement process) we can focus on the humans who are going to be using it as per our human-centricity principle, and we can, using our second principle of diverge–converge, explore different options and scenarios for that space. However, even with all of this we might miss bringing a level of depth, breadth and richness to the project. We could easily miss the latest thinking in neuro architecture that will give us a much deeper view on how certain design cues can be used to modify psychological wellness positively. We might miss the layers and breadth of the future office experience by focusing on the spatial aspects but not the audio or visual aspects. We may not go deep enough with our users to get a true and rich picture of future use of that space. We may not even link the new space with our culture, values and strategy. If we are thinking as designers, then we must actively search for this level of depth, breadth and richness. It is that constant seeking that for me is the core of the destination mindset. A constant nagging about how thorough we have been around something. Have we explored at the right level for this design that we are creating? Have we been holistic enough? Have we tapped into the multiple layers of the experience? My experience tells me that if we seek out DBR naturally then we will find new paths for improvement and innovation beyond what we expected.

By way of example, the FOWI worked with an organisation in the social media sector. The focus of the initiative was to create a more compelling engagement approach that would give this young cohort of people a greater sense of belonging to the organisation. Through deep collaboration and the use of diverge–converge, together we were coming up with some lovely ideas but our gut said we needed some DBR. As it turns out, the group had a broadly held penchant for sci-fi concepts and an incredibly unique approach to the engagement programme emerged—based on what can only be described as friendly, rotund, robotic characters from another dimension! Generating a much more exciting and enticing approach to what could have been a very worthy but dull initiative. Simple advice—be more DBR!

Bottom Line

For your future work world, you are all destination designers. Embrace the design mindset. Recognise that every initiative, programme and strategy across the 3 Ws of work can be elevated to being a 'destination'—something that people will want to spend time on, with and at. Practically, utilise the core principles of human centricity, diverge–converge and DBR consistently. Select a project that you believe could be designed better, adopt the philosophy of Shoshin and redesign it. Select an experiment to really test the redesign's strengths and weaknesses and act on the findings. Congratulations! You are now thinking a little bit more like a destination designer; you will be pleasantly unsurprised by the amount of bad design surrounding you.

BW Darvin

MetaModern Reflective Practice:

Managing Experience,
Sustainability & Transformation

The New York Times Bestseller
7 million copies sold

Jump 4: Book Review

Metamodern Reflective Practice
Best Readz Reader Review
4/5 ☺☺☺☺

—*Camille Nivermin*

It's only 6 months since the publication of *Metamodern Reflective Practice* by B. W. Darvin but it is rapidly becoming the unlikely post-modern 'bible' for leaders disillusioned with traditional rigid management practices that have led to burnout, underperformance and high attrition. Some Gen As (like me), who have found themselves forcefully promoted to leadership positions, are turning their backs on an elevation that is seen these days as a curse and not a compliment. This book could well be the antidote.

The book, more akin to the classic *The Monk Who Sold His Ferrari* than a standard leadership manual, to date has sold over seven million copies. The core idea is based on a deep, holistic and continuous focus on personal and team wellbeing across multiple areas.

One of the key principles in the book that really resonated with me is the idea of leadership as a shared responsibility of the group, with the 'team ambassador' (author's words) providing counselling, wellness advice, spiritual guidance and facilitation support. I enjoyed this book—it opened my eyes to a different way of approaching leadership that still integrates previous leadership theories but comes at it from a very different perspective.

Specifically, the book details the 'Big 8' areas that are key to proper reflective practice:

- Social
- Financial
- Intellectual
- Spiritual
- Environmental

- Occupational
- Emotional
- Physical

These eight areas provide a complete approach to understanding your-self and your team in a truly holistic way. The metamodern bit seems to focus on how to deal with the often-contradictory nature of these areas, and being comfortable with deep diversity, enabling diverse dialogue and encouraging healthy conflict.

Leadership as something holistic and shared by a group of individuals held together by something bigger is an idea that gives me comfort, as someone struggling with the idea of the 'buck falling with me'. Being more of a guide and facilitator-type 'leader' is something I can get on board with! The main reason it doesn't get a full '5 Smilies' is some of the spiritualistic content—might be a little bit out there for some, or is it perhaps that my consciousness hasn't caught up with it yet? Who knows! Highly recommended.

Metawaves

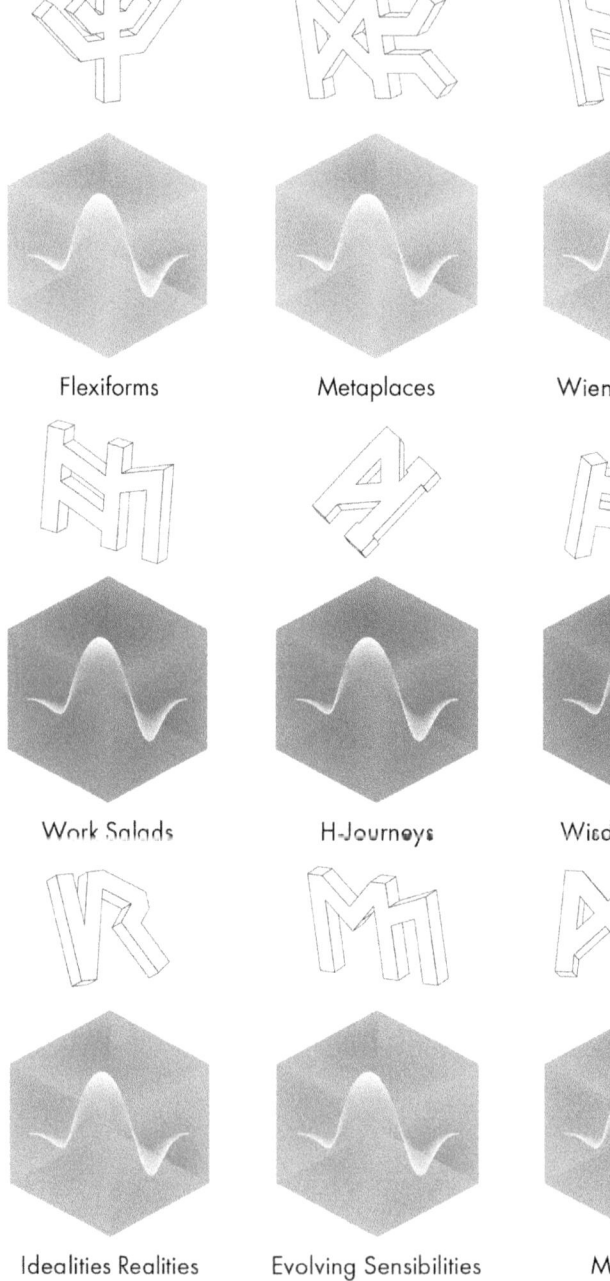

Flexiforms

Metaplaces

Wienie Wonders

Work Salads

H-Journeys

Wisdom Worlds

Idealities Realities

Evolving Sensibilities

Mixing Ms

Welcome to the metawaves! This part focuses on the underlying waves of work change and evolution across workplace, workforce and worktask. The metawaves are jumping-off points, design inputs and inspirations that will help you to reflect on your own working world. The 'meta' bit refers to the fact that they are more than trends. They represent an educated, extended glance towards a vaguely outlined future shore (the 'waves' bit). For the sake of simplicity (and brevity!), there are three Ms for each of the three Ws. Nine metawaves in total. According to various sources, the number 9 is often associated with enlightenment, new adventures and risk taking. It is not in any way serendipitously that we arrived at nine metawaves. Honestly.

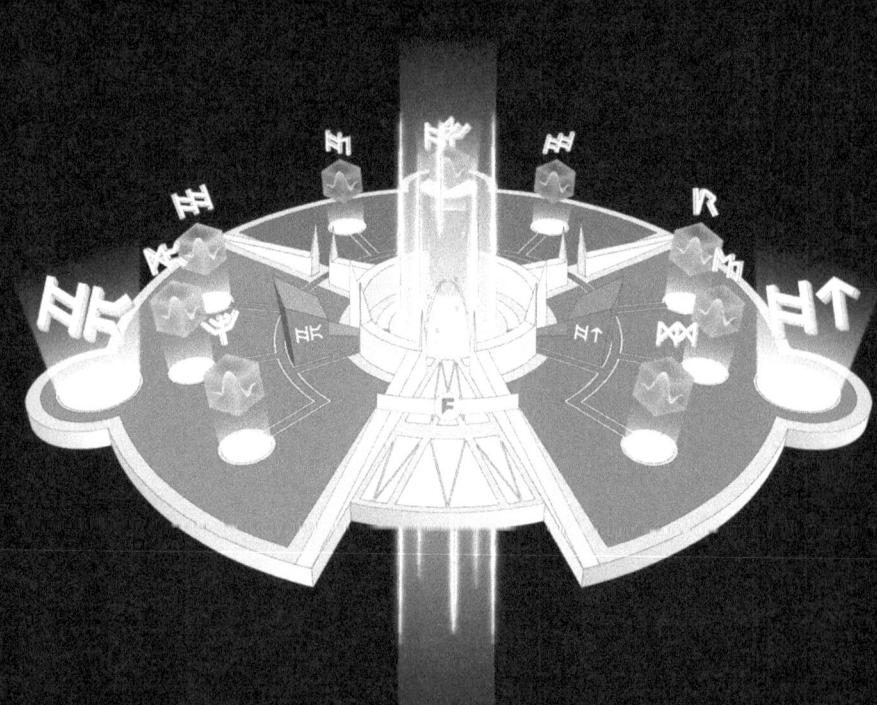

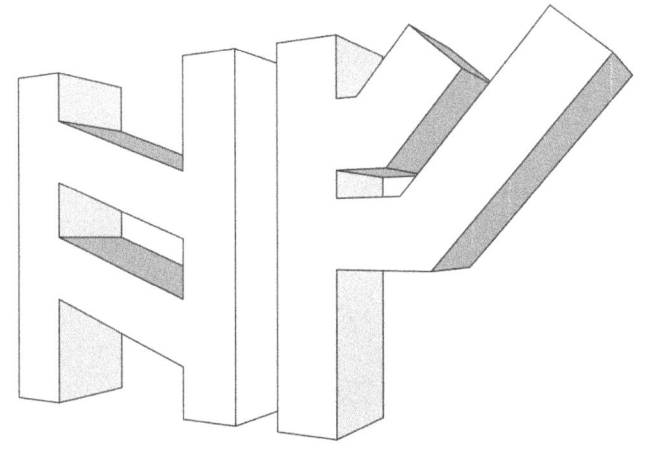

4

Workforce

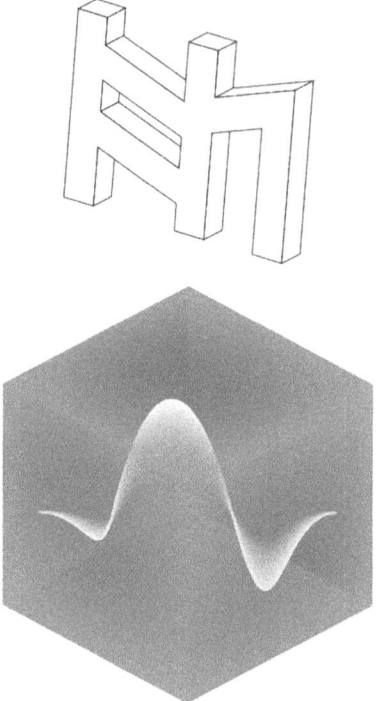

Work Salads

Rolly Crump might not be a name familiar to those outside of certain circles. He was one of the original imagineers who helped Walt Disney create the first true theme park, Disneyland. In his fantastic memoir *It's Kind of a Cute Story* (Crump, 2012), he likens the original Disneyland to a salad. 'From day one, I've always felt that Disneyland was a gorgeous salad because of the ingredients. There is a little bit of something in there for everyone. The attention to detail is one of the most important pieces of it, because there is so much in there. A good example is the little figures in the popcorn wagons. Those little things are the croutons. . . that are in the salad that make it so delicious. I really feel that is why Disneyland was so successful. I hate to say it, but the other theme parks were nothing more than just lettuce and tomato'.

The modern workforce in organisations is best likened to a salad. A mixed salad of different work-type models ranging from permanent employment to gigs. A mixed salad that could potentially offer a 'little bit of something for everyone'. But only some forward-thinking organisations like GE are fully harnessing things like 'crowd' models via their Genius Link platform, in collaboration with UpWork, to get access and insights globally from millions of experts. Lego, and other businesses, are blurring the lines between employee and customer, through co-creation models. Lego's own platform, Lego Ideas (ideas.lego.com/), utilises ideas and concepts from the customer to turn into new products. Uber are utilising the power of their unique work salad in their employer proposition, positioning themselves as a highly viable alternative to more traditional work that offers a level of freedom well beyond traditional measures of flexibility.

To give a sense of the growth of the growth in alternative workforce models, in the United States freelancers generated over $1.5 trillion in income in 2024, with 76 million+ people freelancing. Meanwhile, in India, gig hiring across sectors saw explosive growth, particularly in blue-collar (92%) and project-based roles (38%). In the United Kingdom, the self-employed population stood at approximately 4.38 million in 2025, representing around 13% of the workforce. It is likely that more than one in three of us are exploring a side hustle or passion project that we are in some way monetising. If I think about a subset of my own social circle, at least 40% are working 'for themselves' and 10% are in the process of writing some form of fiction or non-fiction book! In essence, many have already 'resigned' or given up on their dependency with more traditional employment models.

Whilst these new models of work provide many advantages, they are also creating new complexities and emergent challenges. How inclusive should an employer be to their broader blended workforce pool on initiatives like wellness supports? How connected and engaged can a blended workforce be (or need to be) to the core organisation? These are just two of a myriad of questions leaders will face as they try to harness the blend.

In their superb book *Work without Jobs* (2022), Ravin Jesuthasan and John W. Boudreau propose that companies adopt a 'new work operating system that emphasizes the work instead of the job, encourages collaboration between humans and machines, and recognizes the gamut of existing and future work styles like gig, freelance, and contract'. John Winsor and Paik (2024) in his pioneering work on open talent purports that 'by embracing open talent, enterprises can connect with a vast network of people and organisations generating innovative solutions'. It is becoming more and more obvious that we may very well be on the cusp of a new total work-force model that works for many.

The Ideal Work Salad

Wearing our systems architect hat, ideality for an organisation when it comes to the perfect work salad amounts to something like:

- We have access to all the talent,
- possessing all the skills we need,
- exactly at the time we need it,
- with zero legal and compliance risks,
- with zero friction onboarding and offboarding,
- with all possible diversity, inclusivity and social sensitivity fully built in,
- with everyone always aligned with our vision, mission, values and ways of working.

From the perspective of many organisations today, this might seem like a distant dream. But the new models of work, enabled by increasingly sophisticated technology platforms and automated tools, are moving the dial more towards elements of this form of workforce ideality. Making it happen will require harnessing, in a much more connected way, the various forms of the new models of work, and linking them strategically to the diverse goals and needs of different divisions within an organisation.

The Reality—A Long Way Off but Getting There

It is clear the list of work salad ingredients available is growing. Open models, fractional, evolved gigs, platform-based freelancing. It's all happening. But are organisations creating a rich workforce salad or is it a little bit more lettuce and tomato? From multiple clients working sessions and projects via the Future of Work Institute (FOWI) it is obvious that there is an entrenched mental model of the work salad. Generally, this is a moderately empowered, moderately hierarchical approach to the workforce, with a growing use of some mixed employment models (e.g., permanent, temporary and contin-gent). Supplemented by contracting. If other models are used, they are often infrequent and disconnected from an overall workforce strategy. The default approach is still a significant focus on the 'owned' workforce—those employees who spend all their time working with one organisation. The reality is that mindsets need to evolve beyond these relatively narrow mental models. All the ingredients are there to create a truly wonderful work salad. This work salad can provide different forms of advantages depending on need and context.

Even One New Ingredient Creates a Better Salad

In an interview with Flexsource (a leading contingent workforce organisation servicing global clients in Ireland, the United Kingdom and Europe), MD John Twomey feels the real opportunity exists in mixing some of these workforce ingredients together to find new advantages. This approach enables the creation of new career pathways that provide something different to a diverse cohort of current and future employees, as well as giving organisations an ability to open new talent pools, increase flexibility and find new ways to tap into true diversity. He highlights this opportunity by way of a client example within the medical device sector. Their primary workforce model was based on permanent employment. The skills shortage was significant in the areas around the sites they operate in. To paraphrase John, 'the talent tap had run dry'. To deal with this challenge, a temporary workforce model was trialled, designed to align much more effectively with the unique needs of untapped talent cohorts in the locale. This approach led to a large increase in candidates interested in working with the business. The temporary model 'aligned much more effectively with the work/life balance needs of the key talent groups that we had targeted', according to John. More than that, a new talent journey to permanency was created for those employees who wished to work in a more traditional manner. The addition of agile forensic training to empower other talent groups from unexpected sectors has resulted in broadening the talent pool even further. John notes that 'this isn't about selling the dream but educating organisations to think beyond one or two models, and to explore and harness the good and be aware of the bad of multiple models based on the unique talent challenges they pose'.

Outsourcing Isn't Outsourcing Anymore

Suzanne Dolan, MD of Covalen (a European outsourcing organisation) highlights that outsourcing, another ingredient in our work salad, 'used to be very transactional. But this has changed into becoming transformational.

Organisations want a partner, an extension of their workforce, to help them achieve strategic goals'. She notes that whilst the productivity impact of outsourcing models is well documented, the positive workforce impact is often underemphasised. She believes that these types of models provide a level of workforce flexibility that enables rapid scale up and scale down, delivered in a highly professional and compliant way. She also notes that the best outsourcing providers have built strong competencies in reaching and effectively engaging large and diverse talent pools, globally, enabling their client partners to reach new levels of genuine workforce inclusivity.

A Lot of 'Ingredients'

For the modern organisation that is either starting up, scaling up, maturing or finding itself in challenging times, there is a more than decent set of ingredients (see Figure 10) to play with when it comes to crafting the perfect work salad. Thinking broadly about the various ways to utilise these models is key to true strategic workforce innovation. If you are a start-up, can you tap into perhaps a low-cost form of occasional brain trust—a temporary low-cost virtual board that helps enhance your organisation's reputation and provides even small levels of forensic insight and support.

If you are a more mature organisation, does it make sense to utilise more of a gig model for certain specialist support services? A senior leadership group might benefit from the support of some fractional leaders one day per week if moving into a new market, product set or facing a heretofore unencountered challenge that needs a set of more experienced eyes. Considering the multiple ingredients in the work salad is a more sophisticated and nuanced way to think about workforce strategy. It also provides a

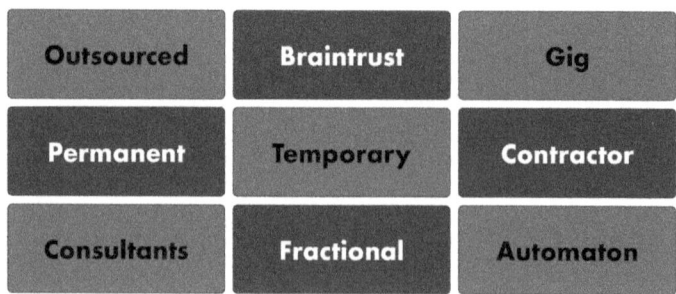

Figure 10   The growing ingredients of the work salad

link to talent that might not have been accessible in the past and makes working with your organisation much more attractive. The number of ingredients will continuously evolve to reflect societal, technological and demographic change. For example, the 'automaton' (referring to anything that can autonomously deliver a task, process or outcome) must be fully in our thinking when it comes to workforce strategy. The same as we may have asked a few years ago 'What is non-core that can be outsourced?', we now must ask 'What is non-core that can be automated?'.

It is likely that organisations' approach to workforce strategy will continue to evolve across several spectrums to fully harness the opportunity and tap into the diverse talent pools needed to attract and retain to thrive.

- **Owned to Open:** Increasing the move away from the traditional core of permanent employment.
- **Mono to Poly:** An increasing variety and diversity of work models used.
- **Static to Dynamic:** A greater focus on enabling the agile use of diverse work models in different and dynamic contexts, times and conditions
- **Disconnected to Integrated:** A better integration of these models into strategic, tactical and operational activity.
- **Pools to Communities:** Creating engaging clubs, ecosystems and communities to keep future potential talent engaged and energised in a much more consumerised way.

Each model has, of course, unique benefits and challenges. Being able to work with all of these models effectively, and often simultaneously, will become a critical competency for organisations. If the current workforce era has been defined by 'solutions' and the use of various partners to provide everything from RPO (recruitment process outsourcing) to MSPs (managed service providers) and BPO (business services outsourcing), then the near-future era, at least as it relates to the workforce, might well be defined by 'strategy', or more precisely 'integrated strategy'—developing an organisation's ability and competence to fully harness and integrate all the models available to them at different times, under different conditions and within evolving contexts.

Questions to help you think

1. What if you tapped into one new work model? What impact might it create?

2. Where is the area that you could quickly apply a new work model?

3. How could you use a new work model to increase the level of diversity in your organisation?

4. What would a new career journey look like using multiple 'ins' across the various work models? How might it work?

5. How might you create a talent community of candidates that is more like a club? How might you engage the community to keep them involved?

6. How might this workforce strategy way of thinking help transform your organisation or business unit strategy?

7. How might you rapidly upskill and validate new model workers lacking key competencies?

8. What area do you believe would gain huge value from a temporary 'brain trust'—be honest!

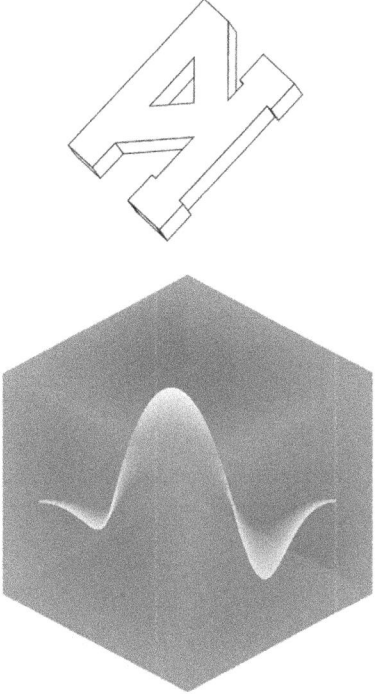

H-Journeys

The Hero

In 1949, *The Hero with a Thousand Faces* by Joseph Campbell was published (Campbell, 1949). It was to become a landmark. In it, Campbell outlines what he calls the 'monomyth'—a universal narrative structure that appears across myths, legends, religious stories and even modern literature and film. The core thesis is that all heroic journeys share a common template, regardless of cultural or historical differences. He identified a universal structure—the hero's journey—which comprises three main parts: departure, initiation and return. It's well known that George Lucas used this very structure to base his epic Star Wars saga on. Campbell also argues that the hero's journey is not just a storytelling formula—it reflects a deep psychological truth. And that the hero's path is in essence an allegory for real life, human self-discovery and development.

These ideas have a deep relevance to the new world of work. Until relatively recently, most of us have followed a well-scripted career journey, overseen and mostly owned by the organisations we work for. In essence it was, and for many still is, less hero journey and more a standardised model of career progression and development geared towards an organisation's success. Now a growing number of people want to be the heroes of their own career journeys, seeking new adventures, a new form of total work experience and crafting success within (but increasingly beyond) the horizons of traditional organisations that can't possibly live up to these hyper-personal and fulfilling experiences. From an organisational standpoint there is an opportunity if not to match these new hero journeys, then at least to move a little closer to re-imagining these career journeys as hero journeys, broadening where they start and end, designing with the needs, emotions and expectations of different users in mind, and with meaningful experience at its core.

Career Crafting

Everywhere we can see examples of individuals crafting their own heroic career paths—self-creating careers or fulfilling long-held passions using the plethora of technologies (including AI), platforms and mega networks now available to us all. Take, for example, 'The Hacksmith' as a case in point (an engineering hero of mine). On his massively subscribed (more than 15 million subscribers) YouTube channel, the team bring fictional, often iconic, objects from comic books, movies and games to life by combining imagination, technology and engineering expertise. Captain America's shield, Iron Man's helmet and even the legendary Star Wars™ lightsaber have all been given the Hacksmith treatment. There is even a touch of the Tony Stark (Marvel's Iron Man) about founder James Hobson.

He and his Hacksmith Industries are a notable example of a new type of hero's journey where passionate individuals have grown side hustles into fully fledged future of work firms (take that alliteration!) thanks to enabling and democratised technologies—including platforms and advanced (and often intelligent) marketing, selling and making tools. We are now in an era where an individual, regardless of how niche their skills and passions are, can monetise their offerings, their stories and their products to equally niche markets via social platforms using precision targeting tools. Combine this with a growing awareness of self, an appreciation of the mega connectivity of the world around us and a greater focus on personal fulfilment, and we have a perfect cocktail for change and disruption.

From Mono to Multi

Conor Lynch, serial digital innovator, entrepreneur and career design expert, thinks very differently about the future of the career ladder. Since launching his first personal brand in 1999, he has seen firsthand the evolution from linear to non-linear careers and now into what he defines as 'multi-linear' careers. These types of careers are different to the zigzag and squiggly careers often referenced as they represent the development of multiple, complementary career activities that are concurrent rather than consecutive. Think of multiple side hustles, projects, collaborations and partnerships with the goal of maximising income and decoupling the mental connection between hours and money. At once an individual may well be in full-time employment whilst supporting a social media side hustle and a sales channel partnership in anything from dog feeders to saunas. The real disruptive jump, according to Conor, is away from a narrowly defined career ladder perspective to what he calls 'The Assets Ladder' (he has penned a book with the same name; Lynch, 2025). Through his work he sees a world where 'workers' can be seekers, partners, owners and multipliers all at once and strategically create their own hero's journeys.

The Evolution of Expectation

Quite simply, our very expectations as individuals have now changed when it comes to work. We have options far beyond the previous generational constructs of what work is and needs to be. We will have the ups and downs of economic cycles that will modify supply and demand balance, but the underlying current of change is towards the talented individual not actually towards the organisation.

At the core of this change is what I call the 'transformation expectation'—an underlying desire for us as unique individuals to do work that is at once a meaningful and passionate experience and transforms us in ways that are very personal to us. We have gone past the work as job and work as career models of thinking. It is very much work as personal experience, work as personal transformation enabled generally by a portfolio of activities. This broadly aligns with the concept of the 'Experience Economy' first posited by Pine and Gilmore (1999). Many people are not 'opting out' per se, but they can now explore avenues and work experiences that make real their own transformation expectations.

The Other Hs

There are two other Hs, beyond 'hero', that we need to consider when it comes to creating career journeys of value for current and future employees. One H is obvious—'human'; the other perhaps not so much—'holistic'. Many are and have been highlighting the need for organisations to become more human in our near and midterm future of work in terms of who we deliver the work to that we do. Lots of books and articles abound on the topic—and there is nothing wrong with the sentiment or the idea. In fact, it is a noble goal. Equally, however, it is a vague concept open to multiple interpretations. From FOWI work with multiple HR leaders as part of ongoing future work world research, when we asked 'What does a "more human" organisation actually mean?', the answers were varied but could be bucketed into a number of key themes, namely: flatter structures and empowerment; a deeper understanding of the human condition; crafting experiences that matter; an evolved approach to leadership; balance, inclusiveness and authenticity; demystified and ethical use of technology; personalisation of the development of the journey; and flexibility as the norm. What was interesting from that research was a recognition of the broad and multi-layered aspects that make up and impact 'the human experience'.

Holistic, at least for our purposes, is perhaps a more useful word than human. The philosophical definition of holistic is 'characterised by the belief that the parts of something are intimately interconnected and explicable only by reference to the whole'. Simply put, it's about connecting the dots and finding the right dots to increase impact at a much higher level. It means broadening our view to recognise as many factors or elements as we can when it comes to, in our case, creating journeys of value.

Holistic in Action

The development and implementation of a more rounded wellness and experience approach highlights the power of 'holistic' in action. Led by FOWI principal and wellness thought leader Elysia Hegarty over a period

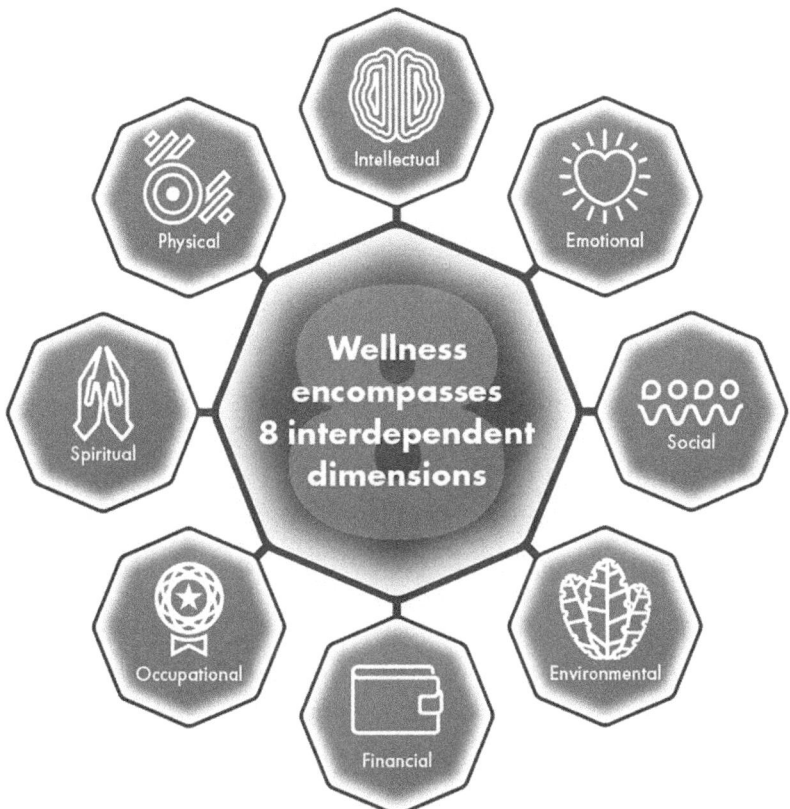

Figure 11   The eight dimensions of total wellness

of two years, FOWI conducted a deep dive on organisational wellness. This research highlighted how a multi-dimensional, holistic approach is necessary across eight dimensions of wellness (see Figure 11) to properly design something of genuine impact.

- **Spiritual Wellness:** Aligning your values and purpose with those of the company.
- **Intellectual Wellness:** Having the ability to respond positively to intellectual challenges and expanding knowledge and skills.
- **Social Wellness:** Maintaining healthy relationships, enjoying being with others, developing friendships, contributing to and feeling part of a team.

- **Vocational/Occupational Wellness:** Preparing for and participating in work that provides personal satisfaction and life enrichment that is consistent with your values and allows for opportunities to advance a career contributing to your skills and talents.
- **Physical Wellness:** Caring for your body to stay healthy now and in the future.
- **Emotional Wellness:** Caring for your mental health, feeling positive and enthusiastic about life.
- **Financial Wellness:** Managing your resources to live within your means, making informed financial decisions and investments, setting realistic goals and preparing for short-term and long-term needs or emergencies.
- **Environmental Wellness:** Understanding how your social, natural and built environments affect your health and wellbeing and demonstrating a commitment to a healthy planet.

Narrow-view programmes can often miss the real levers that can generate impact. If employers simply focus on physical and emotional wellness, they may miss out on vital areas that may also contribute to work-related stress. In our work at FOWI, using a bespoke diagnostic tool we have seen many areas beyond these contribute to work-related stress, such as conflict on the team (Intellectual Wellness), lack of opportunities (Occupational Wellness), personal finances (Financial Wellness) and isolation (Social Wellness).

Even within a business, different departments will have very different needs once we start applying more holistic frameworks to how we deliver work. Figure 12 is an example from an organisation highlighting very different needs—one area had a significant amount of emotional stress and wellness challenges whilst, interestingly, another department had stressors relating to how best to manage finances (a younger cohort of workers were part of that department).

According to Elysia, this research revolutionised her own thinking in understanding that 'once you start researching and doing in a more holistic way you realise there is no end. You must continually seek higher levels of holistic, "connect the dots", thinking. For example, wellness as a concept is really another layer, or set of layers, in an overall employee experience that needs to be better integrated across all parts of the journey. It is still seen in

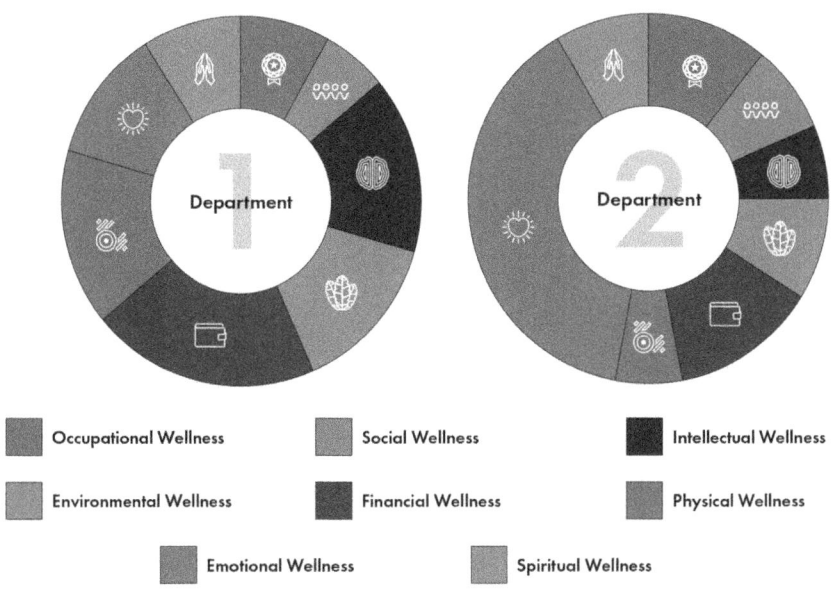

Figure 12 Differences in two departments, one business division

many organisations as a separate event and support-driven set of initiatives. This is linear thinking at best'.

A Thousand Faces, Many Layers

With our destination designers' mindset, we must recognise that we are now dealing with five generations at work and multiple other layers of diversity beyond age. We have a colourful mosaic of opportunities (and potential complexities) to provide more personalised career experiences and journeys for those employees and employee groups. From our work at the FOWI we are seeing only a small (albeit growing) appreciation in some organisations for more individualised designs of personal wellness: specific life-stage needs, targeted diversity and inclusion initiatives and a refocusing of benefits, developmental supports and alternative ways of working to enable people to be at their best at work at various stages of their career.

Without this level of design focus it may well be that soon, many organisations might only be a small part of many people's career journeys. From our own research, many organisations have not even taken the key first step of mapping out in detail career journeys, and key career moments of truth. This is representative of a broader set of missed opportunities to create greater levels of engagement, belonging and loyalty. Any meaningful journey map must be co-created with the people who have been on, are on or will be on that journey. It must also look beyond the process steps and go deep on the emotional element of the journey we are trying to improve, as well as identify key touchpoints in the journey that we can use to 'wow' potential and current employees.

Figure 13 shows an example of a simplified journey map. But mapping the journey is only the start. To make journeys that are memorable and transformational requires a dedicated focus from talent, HR and broader leadership in organisations to ensure success. Creating 'real H' is about being as holistic as possible—creating multi-layered and multi-faceted experiences for the many heroes you are trying to support on their journeys of growth and transformation.

Stages	AWARENESS	CONSIDERATION	CONVERSION	TRANSITION	ACTIVATION
Objective	Raise awareness of the business through multiple channels Engage passive candidate	Drive candidates to engage further with business Drive applications from qualified candidates	Nurture and qualify candidates through to Interview Screen out unsuitable candidates	Final screen of candidate suitability Negotiate with candidate	Onboard candidate to the team
Touchpoint	Online presence Physical and virtual meetings Referral Targeted marketing through social channels	Email Call Physical and virtual meetings Targeted marketing	Conversations Email Screening interviews Assessments Feedback	Reference checks Conversations Medicals Contracts	Handbooks/ Procedures Meetings Pre-boarding welcome pack Welcome events
'Ideal' Emotional Journey	Curiosity Eager to move, Career improvement, Pride, Hopeful	This might be an interesting move that meets my needs	Frustrated if delays or poor experience	Nervous, Stressed (delays), Anxious Eager	Relieved, Hopeful, Excited, Nervous

Figure 13 **A start in mapping journey moments**

Questions to help you think

1. How much of a hero's journey is your organisation's career journey?
2. How holistic is your thinking? Have you considered all the dots? Are you joining the right ones?
3. Have you mapped the journey?
4. How inclusive are your maps? How well do they take the 'thousand faces' into account in those maps?
5. Is inclusive design built into each key stage of the career journey?
6. How well considered are the key moments of magic or truth across those journeys?
7. How well have you built in the emotional aspects of the journey?
8. Could you harness mono to multi thinking and create new options of growth for your employees? Can you harness side hustle and asset creation thinking but within the organisation?
9. How well are you harnessing work salads to be part of top talent's own hero journeys?

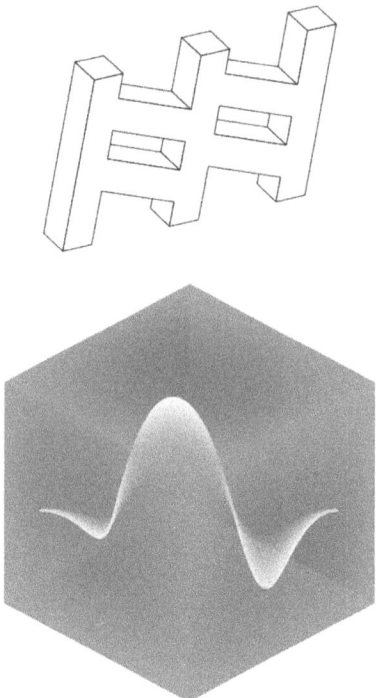

Wisdom Worlds

How many skills do you acquire when you learn to play guitar? As a guitarist, reluctant performer and sometime failed band member, it is a question I often reflect on. It turns out that you learn quite a lot of skills from playing the humble guitar—or any performance instrument for that matter. Having conducted my own deep dive on this one, it comes to about 12 skills—cutting across cognitive, social, physical and emotional domains (see Figure 14). I was genuinely surprised by the skills I acquired on my guitar journey. And in a way this is at the core of the opportuntiy for organisations when it comes to their skills agenda—being fully skills centric and able to see, at scale, a whole skill view of candidates and colleagues.

In fact, when it comes to the future of work and your own future work world, skills and indeed knowledge are a BHIT (a big hairy important topic!). Skills for today. Skills for tomorrow. Skills gaps. Skills that traverse roles and sectors. Skills we (or organisations) don't know we have.

Figure 14 The skills acquired as a perfoming guitarist

The skills-based organisation (developed and popularised by Deloitte). Skills-based hiring. Democratisation of skills. Re-skilling and upskilling. The list goes on and on ad infinitum.

The Importance of a Skills

There is broad agreement about the importance of skills in ensuring societies and organisations are resilient to ongoing change. Nurski and Alcidi (2024) note that 'skills which define labour and human capital, are a central asset for competitiveness'. In 2025, the Union of Skills was launched by the European Union to address critical skills gaps and promote a culture of lifelong learning, underlying the critical importance of skills in regional productivity and, indeed, social cohesion. Hall et al. (2013) notes the innovation rates are higher in skill-intensive firms, while Cammeraat et al. (2024) links higher technical and specialised skills to better productivity outcomes. In many ways there isn't anything new when it comes to the importance of skills but there is definitely a more purposeful focus on the total skills agenda at both national and organisational levels globally. There is a growing recognition of the importance of skills beyond the traditional boundaries of more formal educational qualifications. A whole-skill view of people. Ryan Roslansky, CEO of LinkedIn, speaking at the European Employment and Social Affairs Forum 2025, has urged recruiters to prioritise skills over traditional educational credentials. Ben Mason, CEO of disruptive scale-up Global Bridge, strongly advocates for a shift towards a whole-skills view even at school level—to be inclusive of the breadth of skills unique to every student and create much greater levels of social and employment inclusion.

From an organisational perspective, the opportunity is significant. Creating a wisdom world that has access to incredible skills intelligence, can hire based on skills, validating those skills at scale, continuously upskilling people at pace in enriching and immersive ways, whilst fully harnessing tacit knowledge and insights. It may well be the case that many organisations are a long way away from being a wisdom world. But there are three key pillars of the future of skills in organisations that can be harnessed to get there: experiential, skills intelligence and wisdom now.

Experiential

Immersive technologies, coupled with better hardware and increasing processing power, the emergence of AI-driven learning and development, connected platforms and the reshaping of skills acquisition to novel forms is amounting to a total experiential revolution in how we acquire, use and validate skills. Never before have we had the opportunity to learn in ever more immersive, impactful and enriching ways.

Mersus Technologies—a leader in immersive media and learning and a pioneer in the development of a low-code, accessible approach to generating virtual learning experiences—understands the power of immersion in creating learning experiences that create exponential value. According to CEO Geoffrey Allen, 'when it comes to VR experiences, people expect George Lucas, people expect that level of rich immersion—and every day we are getting closer to being able to do that at scale'. He suggests that just as Gutenberg's printing press revolutionised access to knowledge, immersive media is now transforming how we learn, communicate and operate. He positions Mersus not as a tech company, but as a media company—one that is part of a new epoch where the medium is no longer static or linear, but interactive, spatial and user-driven. Immersive learning experiences are still very much in the early stages of widespread organisation adoption—most learning content still uses a traditional blend of online supported by in-person sessions, and hands-on learning 'on site' in real-world environments. Some of the barriers are due to the current development cycle of getting to a level of quality that is acceptable. Goeffrey points to the validated superiority of immersive VR in generating learning outcomes based on multiple projects they have delivered across specialised industrial and manufacturing environments. He also highlights a 50–80% decrease in training time requirements resulting from using VR.

The immersive element, in essence, needs to become a larger component of the overall approach to organisation-wide learning and development. Moving the blended learning idea to multiple realities, and multi-modal learning experiences based on the appropriateness of each platform to the type and complexity of skills acquisition, development and validation required.

The New Intelligence

Skills intelligence is the new intelligence. Or the new IQ is SQ (skills quotient). Whatever we decide to call it, we need to understand it. Most people don't even know how many skills they have acquired over time—outside of obvious competencies they have trained in—let alone how good they are at those skills, or what skills they need to develop or how to develop them in a way that works for them. If we extrapolate that up to the organisational level of thousands of employees and prospective candidates, we have a whole world of untapped skills intelligence. Until the advent of sophisticated data mining and AI, fully implementing a comprehensive skills intelligence approach would have been impossible. Now, AI can be used across the skills intelligence value chain. AI can be utilised to infer skills. Take my guitar example. If that person plays guitar, they likely have A, B or C skills. AI, gamified and immersive approaches can then be used to validate the level of those skills at scale and suggest avenues for personal skills improvement focus. All of this is putting traditional ideas of recruitment and roles on their head as well.

Insight Sphere, a convergent start-up in the AI and XR space focused on the rapid acquisition of human skills, is at the centre of these changes. CEO Noemi Alvarez highlights how 'AI is moving skills acquisition and development into a more and more dynamic space. It's enabling ultra personalised and continuous learning coupled with real time and precision feedback. The era of the AI revolution for skills is finally hitting the L&D space'. The Insight Sphere communications coach product shows the power of this revolution in convergent thinking—where individuals can improve their communications in context using VR, coupled with AI-enabled L&D backed by models gleaned from best practice (like TED) all bundled into a user-friendly automated coaching tool. Insight Sphere is one example of a growing number of convergent businesses in the L&D space changing the skills value chain.

Going 'Whole Skill'

Ben Mason, CEO of Global Bridge, an edtech scale-up business focused on skills capture and validation for schools, highlights how we 'need to shift towards evidencing broader skills'. He notes the importance of utilising digital credentials to validate the widest possible skills range of students (and by extension, employees). The Global Bridge platform, in a relatively frictionless way, enables students to build a portfolio that becomes a record of the student's development and potential. Ben is excited by how technology, when used properly, can replicate the role of a mentor in identifying hidden talents for organisations, and how it can lead to a greater propensity of 'wildcard' candidates in the recruitment process. Part of this growing technological sophistication will drive a 'greater sense of self-discovery and reflection, linking students and graduates to opportunities they might not even know they are suited for'. By way of example, he highlights how a student with strong maths and music skills might not realise they are well suited to software development, yet data would show a combination like this is a strong predictor of success in that field.

Wisdom Now

If ever a system was following the path of ideality (remember your systems architect mindset), it is L&D. That path is very much about learning systems that can support skills development by themselves, on personalised demand, available anywhere, at any time, fully automated and in ever smaller slices. Micro learning and supporting credentials are growing in popularity. Kapp and Defelice (2019) suggest that micro learning offers numerous benefits, including increased learner engagement, improved knowledge retention and greater flexibility in learning delivery. Insight Spheres communication skills solution is a case in point. Small learning slices, automated coaching, supported by real-time feedback and ultra-personalised improvement paths. It also provides a window into the future use of these types of automated nano-ness when it comes to skills validation. Mersus's Avatar Academy, because of the virtual and immersive nature of the training modules, can provide greater insight and measurement on participants as they undertake various motor and skilled tasks in the virtual environment.

It is likely that the new recruitment journeys will increase the use of automated skills validation using a convergent mix of AI and rich immersion to understand the level of a candidate's skills proficiency. The more we move into the skills-first era at scale, the more needs we will have for ultra-fast, automated validation processes that add to the recruitment experience rather than taking away from it.

Being a wisdom world isn't just about the obvious skills. It's also about knowledge and real world wisdom, and especially how we capture that contextual wisdom that might leave the building when key people leave our organisations. CEO Paul Conneally of Slick+, a rapidly scaling start-up enabling organisations to fully harness tacit knowledge, notes that 'as organisations become more distributed and asynchronous, the spontaneous moments that once facilitated informal and tacit knowledge exchange are disappearing'. Slick+'s platform is designed to enable continuous, on-demand learning by making it easy for employees to record, share and access that tacit knowledge in real time. 'It's about context-specific knowledge—how things are done in your organisation, by your people, in your culture and disseminating that wisdom in more accessible, rich forms like short-form video'. Relying on documentation, presentations and older forms is not enough to make knowledge work for organisations. He notes that the capture of that wisdom must also be simple, immediate and valuable. And that wisdom must be available anytime, anywhere and in the most relevant form. Slick+, Mersus and Insight Sphere are examples of the new wave of organisations that understand not just the value of knowledge, but also the importance of using a rich, multi-layered experience to make it enticing and engaging for employees.

Like many of their peers, their future horizons will be about understanding how advances in enabling technologies like AI can further empower and connect employees and make real the promise of everywhere, all at once, wisdom.

Questions to help you think

1. How much of a wisdom world have you built?
2. Do you have a full skills view of your employee base, or your broader work salad?
3. How well are you truly integrating more immersive approaches to accelerating skills acquisition and application?
4. To what extent have you integrated 'skills first' into your hiring practices?
5. How close are you really to a skills-based organisation? Why would it make sense or not to get there?
6. How are you evolving the role of your L&D teams to focus on experiential and multi-modal learning?
7. To what level are you harnessing skills diversity in projects?
8. How are you enabling ideality for your employees when it comes to learning?
9. How are you utilising AI at scale to infer, validate and support skills?
10. How are you capturing and harnessing the tacit skills and knowledge prevalent across your organisation?
11. How well are you tapping into broader skills ecosystems at organisation and country level to create a meaningful skills strategy?

Disposable Workers

Jump 5: Disposable Workers

Extract from interview with Matt Morrison—a self-styled 'disposable worker'

Just as we are about to chat, Matt, a highly respected and seasoned strategist with a background in the fast-moving consumer goods (FMCG) sector, receives a notification on his phone. He has been asked to join a four-person 'D-team' to deliver a two-week remote project for an up-and-coming nootropics shake business. He knows two of the team already, having worked with them previously on a few 'nano projects' as he calls them. Matt is one of over 40 thousand highly skilled workers whose main revenue comes from being part of 'D-teams' (disposable teams). These are very short-lived teams (often for less than a day but more often two to six weeks) that come together to deliver specialist projects, remotely, all over the world. Some 'nano projects' can be as short as a 3-hour facilitation with a company team needing a different voice to bring them clarity. All of this is made possible through DISp—the platform that is the enabler of this vibrant and highly motivated community. I asked Matt, an early adopter, what attracted him to this way of working, which seems to build on the good and bad of the previous wave of freelancer and gig working models.

> It ticks two boxes for me: Freedom and Fulfilment. I can do projects when I want them, and I can decide the kinds of teams and projects I want to be part of (and like). I can't remember the last shitty project I worked on—a far cry from when I was a junior consultant clocking in and doing all sorts of crap I had no interest in.

But does this way of working not come with risks? What if the projects don't come and you get a lean month. What happens then, I ask Matt.

> There is no doubt about it, it's a different way of working and it doesn't work for everyone. I have a high tolerance for risk, which helps. You need to have put the time in and know what you're about. You need to work hard on your brand on the platform and really focus on delivering your part of the D-teams,

otherwise you will find yourself with very little work. I'm established now and I'm on several long-standing D-teams (called Reunions in the community lingo) that will come together to work on four or five projects a year. All told, I can have a portfolio of projects in the high twenties for a given year. Summer is my 'no time'—between July and August I don't work.

I probe Matt further and ask why the DISp community works where others have failed.

A lot of people I work with on the D-teams will highlight the obvious— many registered organisations on the platform that trust the D-teams, a long track record of good case studies coming out of the community and an amazing project delivery and engagement platform. But I think it's the mindset that is the key difference. It feels like a true collective, and the business model helps that: 30% of any D-team revenue is a success fee that is shared by the members. It's like a delivery dividend and even for that short period of time there is serous ownership over the collective work. It's also so immediate. Deliver a four-week project and the money and the success fee is in your account within a week.

Chip Keen, CEO of ShakeN—the nootropics shakes company (and one of Matt's clients)—is an active user of D-teams across various projects. According to Chip:

The D-team thing worried me a bit at the start. I had spoken to a few other CEOs on the network, and they recommended them to me. We are still in scaling mode so we can't afford high-end consultancy and execution support, but we still need proper expertise to help us grow. The first D-team we used was on a market-entry strategy for Sweden. They were fantastic. Made up of a diverse group—a Swedish expert in on-the-go foods, a Canadian strategist in the FMCG sector, an Indonesian with a background in selling functional foods in Europe and an Irish brand and market entry architect. Suddenly, we found ourselves with a team of A-list stars. In relative terms, the six-week project was great value and brought our business to the next level. We now use the D-teams a lot. Not all our experiences have been great but by and large the results are always better than 7/10. One of the things that I love is the tool on the DISp platform that uses AI to link our briefings to a pool of diverse and global talent from unexpected backgrounds and expertise.

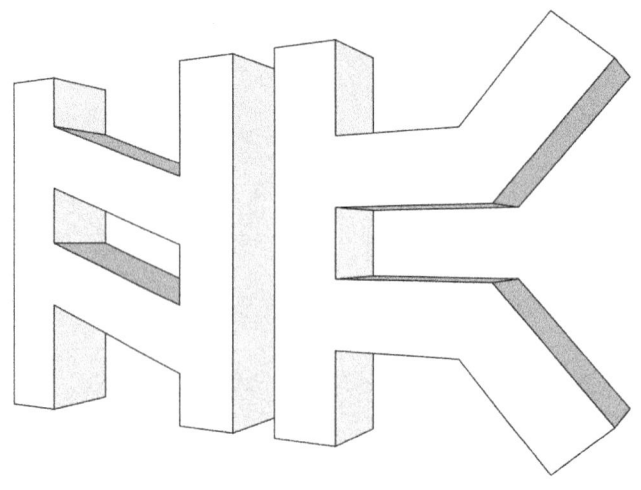

5 | Workplace

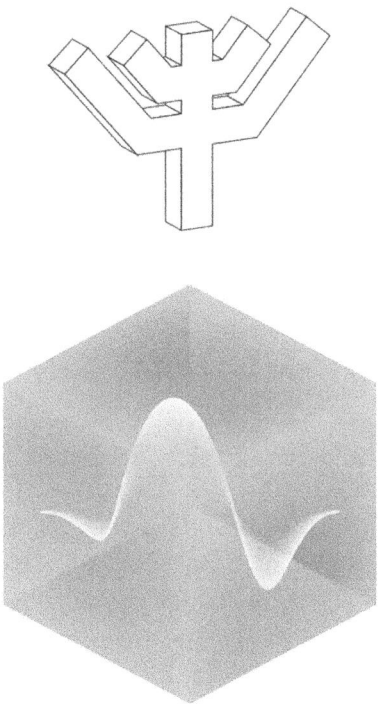

Flexi Forms

Research from the Future of Work Institute (FOWI) has highlighted that one in four people will not even consider a job without a level of flexibility built into the role. Further supplementary research on the changing expectations of work and life programme 2025 from FOWI, covering 1,600 employees across Europe, highlighted that more than 70% of us are availing of at least one form of flexible working. Many organisations have now deployed fully formed flexible working policies. Our places and how we use them, as much as how we work, are now flexible. Yes, there will be those with more of a red/orange mindset (remember your societal whisperer mindset) who will harken back to a 'golden age' (golden age thinking more like) of the five-day week in a physical office. These will always bag the big headlines. But if we look deeper at actual practice, organisations are now harnessing a more flexible form of working.

This flexi form is creating new challenges (and opportunities). There is an emerging two-tier, or two-level, system, with those in offices offered significantly more flexibility than those in other environments like frontline healthcare, construction and manufacturing, who are often excluded from these types of flexible working opportunities (The Guardian, 2025). Yet flexi forms can help decrease congestion, improve the environment, people's wellbeing (in some cases) and help re-use smaller office spaces. This is not a question about 'getting people back to the office'—a wrong solution for a vaguely defined problem. It is about how organisations can integrate flexi forms into the way they do things and re-think the physical, digital and virtual spaces to improve the total experience for their employees. Those organisations—especially in traditionally non-flexible sectors—that make new flexi forms a key part of their employer value proposition may enable a key competitive advantage in their sectors talent race.

Going Deeper on the Flexi Form

The FOWI research (see Figure 15) went deeper to explore the types of flexible working arrangements that are being made available by employers. Overall, we found that many are providing a mix or portfolio (more than three) of different flexible arrangements. For example, Cpl's (a large talent business) approach to flexibility includes dedicated hybrid days, with bank

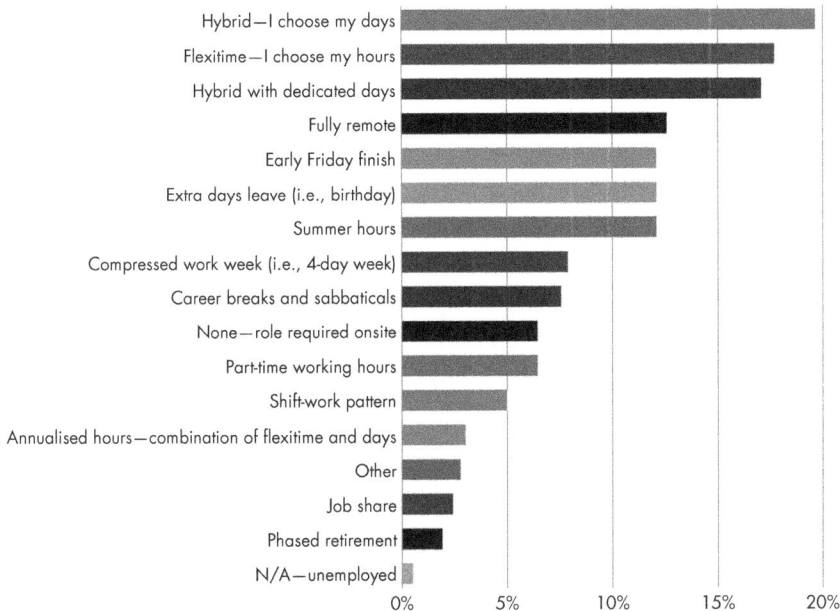

Figure 15 Most frequently used flexible ways of working

holiday early finish Fridays and the provision of career breaks dependent on numerous factors. Whilst some new research is highlighting work/life balance as more important than compensation, our research shows it is still less important than compensation but flexible working is by far the most important benefit across all generations.

The predominant mode of flexibility provided to employees (more than 54%) is centred on hybrid, which predominantly has a 3/2 or 2/3 split (home/office). Interestingly, those working fully remotely approximated 12% and more than 7% avail of a compressed work week—highlighting a greater emergence of these 'next-generation' working arrangements. These findings correlate broadly with other research on the topic. Hybrid work remains the most common arrangement (44%) among EU employees in roles that can also be performed remotely. Workplace-only roles trail at 41%, reflecting a 5% growth over the last year, according to Eurofound's latest *Living and Working in Europe* report (Eurofound, 2024). Fully remote positions across the bloc are in steady decline, dropping sharply from 24% to 14% between 2022 and 2024.

The Flexibility Advantage

Many of the organisations we work with at the FOWI are at the point in their own flexible evolution where they are starting to question or at least reflect on the long-term benefits of a hybrid approach. Commentary generally focuses on two related questions: Can we stand over the good conscientiousness of our employees when they are not as visible? and Has our hybrid approach driven improved (or conversely, negatively impacted) productivity?

There is now a growing body of studies—more sophisticated and nuanced than the early studies in this area—that overwhelmingly highlight the benefits of a more flexible, hybrid model. One of the most recent, useful studies, conducted by Nicholas Bloom, a Stanford economist, centres on an experiment with over 1600 workers at Trip.com—a Chinese online travel agency (Bloom, 2024). The research found that employees who work from home for two days a week are just as productive as fully office-based colleagues. Resignations due to the hybrid schedule fell by 33%.

From a broader context, flexibility can enable employers to tap into a much more diverse workforce. In a 2023 (and still relevant) study from the UK's Commission on Hybrid and Remote Work, 51% of businesses said offering hybrid roles increased their ability to hire people from different regions, 53% said the same about hiring parents or caregivers and 42% for hiring those with a disability (Commission on Hybrid and Remote Work, 2023). From our own research, hybrid working should be seen as a potential strategic lever when it comes to creating a differential advantage over other talent competitors and is a key part of a modern employer's value proposition.

An interesting study by Chang (2025), examining flexible work arrangements across a select group of globally influential organisations, found that these strategies significantly improve market adaptability and productivity whilst also enhancing employee satisfaction and organisation loyalty. An interesting aspect of Chang's work is his emphasis on the value of flexible work arrangements in achieving SDGs (Sustainable Development Goals). This work points towards a more holistic way of thinking about both the strategic and operational value of flexibility.

Cpl: A Case in Point

Cpl Group—a European talent solutions and recruitment company, and part of Osi International—is a good example of an organisation harnessing the new flexi forms both in terms of working practices and in thinking about the physical office space. The organisation provides several different flexible working mechanisms—primarily around the two/three-day hybrid working split. This is supplemented by other flexible offerings like early finish Fridays on bank holiday weekends and an extra day off for people's birthdays. The physical office space HQ at any time can only host about a third of Cpl's one thousand-strong workforce and provides fully flexible desk working. The space has been designed primarily to support collaborative working, with multiple areas for group and client interactions. A number of casual refreshment areas support ad hoc conversations.

As with all things, there are many different versions of flexi forms—some placing a different type of emphasis on the role of physical space and proximity. FOWI worked with a company in the consumer electronics space that drove a commitment to smaller 'spoke' somewheres—where everyone had access to a smaller spoke office to ensure cultural and colleague cohesion, moving away from the idea of the 'one HQ to rule them all' approach. You may even want a temporary somewhere for a short and designated space of time—think outposts and popups.

The Flex Form: Exciter and Expected—It Depends!

In the 1980s, Professor Noriaki Kano developed the now relatively famous (at least in product and marketing circles) Kano model that characterises product features into five types based on how customers perceive them. To keep it simple (apologies in advance to Professor Kano), let's keep the focus on the three 'needs' that Kano defines: basic needs, performance needs and unexpected needs. Basic needs are something a customer, or employee for that matter, expects. It might, for example, be a decent wage—equivalent to or above the minimum wage. Having it doesn't increase satisfaction but not having it increases dissatisfaction. Performance needs are needs such that, the more of them you provide, the more satisfied the customer or employee is. Think about your smartphone. The longer the battery lasts, the higher the level of satisfaction. Then there are the unexpected needs. Features or exciters that surprise the customer or employee. Not having them doesn't decrease satisfaction but having them creates an unexpected form of delight. This might, for example, be an unexpected one-off £2,000 payment to employees prior to Christmas. What is interesting is that in general, things that are exciters over time become performance needs and then basic needs. This model neatly explains the dynamics of flexible working. In a way, COVID created an exciter—100% time working from home. Totally unexpected. This, in turn, resulted in a performance expectation around flexi form ways of working—when things returned to relative normality, some companies continued with high levels of flexibility and some didn't, creating a mixed bag of satisfied employees and dissatisfied ones. It is relatively safe to say, without fear of too much contradiction, that flexi forms of working are becoming more like a basic need. Once you have experienced the 'feature', not having it has a disproportionately negative impact on satisfaction. It is the reason why in many studies, including our own, flexi form models are right up there with remuneration, seen now as more than a benefit, but THE benefit. If we add a broader cultural context onto this, or more precisely the country norms of flexi form working, then we find a mixed-current reality. A Eurofound study (Eurofound, 2024) found that in countries like Finland, Germany, Ireland and the Netherlands, most workers are allowed to work from home fully or partially, with rates close to or over 70%. Whereas Cyprus, Greece, Croatia, Portugal and Italy are some of the least flexible countries, and many people never or very rarely are allowed to work from home. I'd argue that in countries with high levels of flexi form working, flexibility is now a basic need and in those with low levels, flexibility could be the exciter an organisation needs. A killer employer value feature that could create a major differentiator for an organisation attempting to attract and retain the best talent. The same concept applies to those organisations working in sectors with traditionally low utilisation of flexi form working. For example, property developer BAM, in a sector not normally associated with flexible working, first piloted flexible working schemes in 2019 and has since expanded them. With a focus on realistic flexibility like different starting hours, different finishing hours and so on, it is a statement of intent that even in organisations with high physicality requirements, flexi forms are possible.

Conversely, in those countries (and organisations) that have a predisposition towards flexi form working, any push away from existing levels of flexibility might have a disproportionately negative impact on employee satisfaction, loyalty and retention. In those countries and organisations, perhaps work salads—fully integrating and providing various employment models—may offer the next jump in flexi form. Time and tide will tell.

Fully Remote Organisations

Whilst the predominant mode of flexi form is working within some form of hybrid model, there are organisations like Git Lab, Automatic, Deel and Cedar that are remote only. An ONS study (2025) in the United Kingdom highlighted that 18% of people surveyed work exclusively from home. The U.S. Census Bureau (via the American Community Survey) in 2023 reported that the share of workers who 'usually work from home' was approximately 13.8% of the US workforce. These remote-first models provide several advantages, including access to 'all' of the global talent pool, significant cost reductions and many of the advantages already highlighted by the flexible part of hybrid models. As with all new systems remote-only companies face their own, novel challenges, often solved using collaborative technologies, work based on outcomes, a high focus on communication, engagement and wellness, and selective but high-impact physical proximity and presence through offsites, retreats and other mechanisms.

Wearing our system architect hat, does this remote-first/only way of working represent the most likely future of how we are going to work in the 10- to 15-year future? New collaborative and virtual technologies, the seismic shift AI will bring in terms of hyper-productivity, new generations that are digital and virtual natives, a growing number of people taking alternative multi-linear career paths and working from anywhere, might suggest we are thinking about this world of flexibility from the wrong way round. Using the principle of ideality it might suggest that the remote-only model, whilst it has its problems, could generate greater cost, productivity, access and 'belonging' value in the long term. Perhaps, just perhaps, the office-only, office-plus-other-place flexibility working models are merely a jumping-off point for this emerging reality. As Ralph McTell sings, 'it's a long way from there (Clare) to here' and it is more likely, at least in the short term, that we will see a greater formalisation and level of control asserted over flexi form working and a continued melting pot of multiple forms of different models.

Questions to help you think

1. If you are already using flexi forms of working, what would more of it look like?
2. If you are in a challenging environment, what is a flexi form that would work for you? What's your version?

3. If you have recently thought about altering your flexi form, have you fully understood the potential 'Kano' impact?
4. How might you introduce different flexi forms across different times/days, under different conditions, in different contexts?
5. How might you harness flexi forms in low-flexibility contexts and use them as a key differentiator for talent?
6. How might changes in flexi form impact people in the context of Kano's model?

Meta Place

There's a lot of talk about the multiverse. It's exciting and it conjures up images of *Ready Player One* (the book, not the movie) and all sorts of exciting potential. Like many, I have had the pleasure of donning a VR headset and interacting with haptics and some interesting (sometimes not great) educational and entertaining immersive content. I have also interacted with various augmented reality-based games. But let's be honest, for all the sales speak and big talk, we are still some distance away from a fully functioning multiverse. For this metawave I'm interested in a more likely near future, the 'meta place'. Specifically, how can we start thinking about (and creating) our workplaces in a more fluid, multi-dimensional way across the physical, digital and virtual realms and optimise our work appropriately for each of those realms.

There is a burgeoning flow of new start-ups that fully utilise the unique characteristics of each place using a convergent mix of different approaches that can drive higher levels of engagement, interest and impact. Start-ups like Centrical, which leverages a convergent mix of AI and gamification to drive performance and motivation through personalised coaching, real-time performance tracking and a culture of recognition. Its customisable platform features engaging game narratives like car races and treasure hunts, competitions, personal challenges and even a virtual store for redeemable rewards. Insight Sphere, a start-up in the communications development space, recognises the unique value of (in combination with best-practice communication frameworks with sophisticated AI tools) putting the user in a virtual environment that is a good proxy of their physical workplace, enabling practice without the fear of real-world failure.

Large organisations like Cisco and their Global Sales Experience highlights the potential of a meta-place approach to employee engagement. Employees aren't just passive participants in a virtual meeting, but active players in an alternative-reality game. Collaborating and exploring the benefits of company tools effectively boosts awareness and adoption (GPJ, 2022). Best Western immerse employees in avatar-based training simulations, where they navigate realistic customer service challenges and hone problem-solving skills, boosting confidence and performance. Salesforce's gamified sales platform contains challenges, progress bars and leaderboards, igniting a spirit of competition and collaboration and boosting motivation and performance (Malik, 2022).

Younger Generations and the Sense of Place

It could be argued that the next generation of workers are already thinking and doing in a meta-place way. A 2023 European Youth Forum study found that 63% of European teens feel more emotionally connected to online communities than their local environments (Youth Forum Europe, 2023). Generation Alpha is growing up in a world where digital and physical realities are often seen as inseparable. They are interacting with AI, voice assistants and immersive technologies from early childhood. Manurung et al. (2024) note that Gen Z's social life today is very different from previous generations. In many instances, the virtual social life for this generation is as important as their life in the 'real' world. It might not be too far of a stretch to say that the younger generations are not just 'digital natives' but are 'virtual' natives too. The future workplace will have to reflect these preferences and harness a more meta-place way of thinking.

Meta-Dimensional Thinking

In a way, we are currently prisoners of our own mindsets when it comes to thinking about the workplace in a 'meta-place' way. A few years ago, I completed a certificate in immersive storytelling and what really struck home was how linearly I thought about using space and multi-layered environments to engage. Without realising it, I was thinking one-dimensionally in a three-dimensional world. Current thinking about 'place' is often one-dimensional. And this isn't surprising. For many of us, the meta pace is still something new. And the current barriers to learning—or at least understanding—the value of virtual worlds, gamification and immersive storytelling can be high. Geoffrey Allen, CEO of Mersus Technologies, an early innovator in immersive VR in people performance and development, envisions a future—not too far from now—where these barriers will be dismantled. Where young talent—without formal degrees—can rapidly build immersive apps for multiple uses across onboarding, learning and beyond, rapidly using low-code, low-barrier models. He tells stories of apprentices and interns in Mersus who've gone from novices to creators relatively quickly, emphasising the importance of belief, mentorship and imagination in this new multiverse world. He also highlights that although VR training in highly sensitive areas has gained ground, many still don't fully understand the impact that this type of 'virtual-place' learning can have on employees' speed of learning, its ability to overlay real-time wisdom and the real-world readiness it can give to employees beyond more traditional learning approaches. Virtual reality and virtual places have been around for a while but even so, it is a field that is still evolving, with new areas of application emerging daily.

There is an opportunity to think differently and ask ourselves: What meta place do we want to design that empowers our people and optimises different types of work wherever they are in physical, digital or virtual space?. There are things that each of these realms can uniquely do. Need to process an invoice? A great digital platform makes sense. Need a compelling experience that helps you immerse into a building that hasn't been built yet? Fantastic. Virtual all the way. Need to storm the team and get to the heart of things? A physical hub meeting is surely the way to go.

Harnessing Meta Place: Sandyford Business District and the Digital Twin

Sandyford Business District, an innovative, collaboration-focused business district in South Dublin, Ireland, is embracing a meta way of thinking about the now and next of their future 'place'. Using a comprehensive digital-twin model, stakeholders, business owners and residents can envisage new ways of how the district can be planned, and how this will impact day-to-day living and working. According to Ger Corbett, CEO of the district, this digital representation 'fundamentally alters the way that we think about the district's future plans and aids us and our stakeholders as a key decision-making and support tool'. In further discussions he highlighted how access to real-time data and connected devices will enable greater clarity on how the district is used every day by workers and residents and, interestingly, deeper insights into things like environmental footprint and impacts of activities in the district. As part of future developments, the underground utilities network will be incorporated in the digital twin. This critical layer will enhance the model's ability to support infrastructure planning, maintenance coordination and emergency response, ensuring a more resilient and efficient urban environment.

Meta Place, Meta Work

An imaginative meta view of the workplace should consider not just the three realms of physical (office, hubs, other physical spaces), digital (platforms/workflow) and virtual (for our purposes, augmented/virtual reality) but also the work types that will be conducted. There are four work types that we need to consider when designing and optimising for the meta place.

- **Process Work:** Repetitive work with a high level of task similarity—in some instances, this may represent a large or predominant portion of an employee's work focus. The work may still be complex but has a level of consistency in process (i.e., mortgage-approval processes).

- **Project Work:** Work based on delivering small, medium or large projects—things like R&D types, strategic projects and other tasks would sit under this work type. Projects with a finite period.
- **Purpose Work:** Work related to building culture, collaboration, engagement of teams or communities, social or sustainable-type work.
- **Growth Work:** Work related to validating and developing skills, applying skills, assessing performance either in group or self settings.

Whilst these work types aren't meant to be definitive, by putting both together we get a useful meta working grid with work realms on the side and work types on the top. A simple model to help us think in a meta-place way. A working profile for an employee could, for example, look like Figure 16 in the not-so-distant future (and in some organisations, this is already a reality—at least in part) (white means no use of that realm, yellow (light shade) some use, green (dark shade), lots of use).

Many of us are now working in a much more meta-place way. Most of us work on one or more digital platforms. Many of us conduct virtual (albeit platform-based) sessions and meetings daily. However, are organisations maximising the use of these meta places for their teams and the type of work that needs to be delivered? Taking a key process like onboarding, for example, and using our systems mindset, have we explored how the different realms might be optimised for each stage of onboarding? How might we, for example, use a virtual realm experience to assess skills during the validation stage in rapid time (growth work)? Taking another example, we might have a freelance cohort that we need to rapidly integrate into project work.

	Process Work	Project Work	Purpose Work	Growth Work
Physical				
Digital				
Virtual				

Figure 16   Meta working in the meta place

Fortal Virtual Workspaces is an example of a start-up finding new opportunities in a working world that needs to rapidly enable different worker types utilising virtual workspaces. Raj Bhalla, Fortal CEO, sees a growing need to more fully harness virtual workspaces and massively decrease activation times for the new breed of freelance expertise. Fortal enables workers to rent 'virtual' workspaces with a single click that enable real-time collaboration in a third, neutral place and give them access to thousands of tools. He emphasises, in line with the work of the FOWI, how the cultural shift driven by the younger generations is leading to new ways of working and a greater requirement for solutions like Fortal that prioritise frictionless and boundaryless integration across organisations and teams alike.

Questions to help you think

1. What is your meta-place strategy?
2. What types of work could be most optimised for each of the meta-place realms?
3. If you were to create a new attraction experience for Gen Zs or Alpha, what would it look like?
4. What process might you select to trial a meta-place approach?
5. What one element of training could be made more compelling using immersion, gamification or AI?
6. How might you do that first day of induction in a virtual place and why would it make sense?
7. Are digital places being used to the maximum of their features? Do your employees even know what those features are?
8. What if we did that next series of employee and customer engagement events in a new, more immersive digital space? What might it look like?
9. What processes does it make sense to physically, digitally or virtually remix?
10. How might a meta-place approach help optimise the use of different worker types?

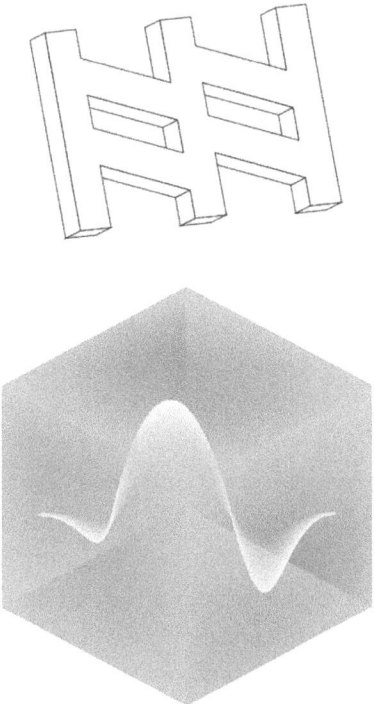

Wienie Wonders

> 'As virtual and physical environments evolve, they will need to better meet the needs of people and customers. There will be a demand for the physical environment to create meaningful experiences & enable connections'.
>
> *Anonymous HR Leader, FOWI Lab on Workplace*

For those of you in the know, 'wienie' is a shorthand, slang description of a hot dog (a Wiener). But for our purposes, as it relates to one of our waves, a 'wienie' is something more interesting. Something that comes from a legend—Walt Disney. The story goes that Walt Disney (during the development of Disneyland) would come home from work, open the fridge and take out two hot dogs. He noticed that his pet dog would follow him wherever he went in hopes of getting one of them as her treat. He applied the

same 'wienie' idea to his first theme park as he needed something that people in the park would naturally be attracted and drawn to (and follow like
his dog!). Sleeping Beauty's Castle at the original Disneyland is a 'wienie'.

From an architectural perspective, a 'wienie' is 'a visual icon that causes
people to gravitate naturally towards a location'. An easier way to say that is
that it's a visual magnet. It's something that catches your eye and draws you
towards it. From a workplace perspective, is your physical workplace a true
'wienie'? Pine (2024) has written about office place as flagship, and transformation architects have gone deep on the idea of place and organisations.
At the FOWI we speak about the destination workplace. And we use this
phrase purposefully. Borrowing from the tourism arena (and subsuming
multiple definitions), a 'destination is a place worthy of an extended stay, a
place that is a reason for visiting a country or area, often tapping into all the
senses and has special attractions for the needs of diverse guests'. All point to
the same general idea—the new workplace is more than just a place. It can
be a destination that is desirable, interesting and supports new ways of collaboration, innovation and understanding for different and diverse employees.

In 'lab workshops' on workplace conducted by the FOWI, which
included various leaders from a diverse set of organisations, the idea of 'wie-
nies, destinations, hubs and "more than an office"' were explored. Some
core themes emerged, including the future role of the physical office or
space in an age of flexibility, the importance of user centricity and the idea
of workplace as everywhere.

In relation to the role of the physical space, the idea of the office as
more a diverse 'hub' and a place for deep social collaboration, a place where
the 'important meetings need to happen', emerged as key concepts. Others
imagined the hub concept as a 'park and ride' for employees, with an ability
to be there from time to time, with smaller offices possibly becoming the
norm. Others saw the physical hub potentially as a brand and cultural
immersion centre, where individuals could re-engage with the brand, the
culture and the DNA of a business or in some instances act almost like a
'health club', where employees might recharge in a group or individual setting. All agreed that there is an opportunity to bring new ideas and thinking
to the concept of the physical office, its integrated design and its use.

As part of these lab sessions it was highlighted that for many the workplace cannot change—those involved in manufacturing, for example, will see

greater automation and connectivity but their workplace for the most part will still be 'physical'. Most agreed, however, that there is both an opportunity and a real need to evolve the role of physical spaces within organisations over the coming years.

As the workplace is becoming more of a meta place, another core theme discussed was the opportunity to create user-centred and personalised experiences that until recently weren't possible. The idea of being able to tap into global expertise, harness new forms of virtual collaboration, learn from other industries and better meet the needs of an increasingly diverse workforce were discussed.

More Than a Place

Companies like Lego are at the leading edge of re-thinking and re-imagining the physical workplace. In what seems like a full-circle moment, Lego bricks were frequently[1] used to capture and evolve ideas for their new Lego headquarters. The building, which broke ground in 2024, will have six overlapping modules featuring play zones and atriums and a 'PlayWay' that moves through neighbourhoods and connects people and functions. Green spaces will be used to maximise natural light and creativity and there is a big focus on sustainability. TravelPerk, an organisation in the travel booking industry, has created a 'place with inclusivity in mind' (Blair, 2023). Their offices span five above-ground floors with relatively fewer desks (all sit/stand) and more open spaces. A wellbeing room, a gym and terraces on every floor provide employees with diverse spaces to work from and allow them to take breaks in more comfortable areas. What's interesting about TravelPerk's unique offices is the fact that the design is centred around a core theme—'the journey in real life'—and each space is designed to immerse employees in an experience related to that journey.

ATI: Rethinking Place

ATI (Accountant Technician Ireland) is a highly innovative, forward-thinking organisation that has fully embraced the idea of 'the physical office space' as something that needed to be re-invented for the new era of work. ATI is not a large organisation and as such highlights the universality of thinking about place as a purposefully designed 'wienie'. According to

COO Gillian Doherty, 'The organization has moved away from the traditional "headquarters" model. The physical space is no longer just a place to work—it's a flexible, evolving environment that supports collaboration, creativity, and community'.

At ATI, the term 'office' has been deliberately abandoned in favour of 'hub' or 'collaboration hub', signalling a cultural and functional shift.

The space is now used in multiple contexts, including flexible working for ATI team members, delivering event programmes, hosting speaker series, training sessions and social events. The design focuses on hybrid, mixed use—combining formal auditoriums with informal welcoming areas. A studio space has been created to amplify voices from the community and the business world. All these initiatives aim to position the hub as a place of wisdom at the centre of a community of practice. This mixed-use approach allows for agility—programmes can be launched quickly, and the space can be adapted to different needs.

A major insight of the changing idea of place is the critical importance of in-person induction. Remote onboarding had led to disconnection and a lack of team cohesion. The organisation now ensures that new hires are onboarded when leadership is present, fostering social integration and a sense of belonging. Training is peer led, with teams delivering sessions on products, processes or compliance. This bottom-up approach enhances engagement and ownership.

From a cultural perspective, Gillian highlighted the critical importance of integrating new language with new ideas of place. 'Terms like "town hall" have been replaced due to their hierarchical or outdated connotations. The space is described as democratic, where everyone feels they have a voice and access to leadership. This cultural shift is reinforced by the physical layout—open seating, no reception desk and informal gathering areas reduce barriers to communication. So far, the transformation has had both strategic and emotional benefits, including a greater feeling of pride and ownership of the space, a greater connection with the external member community and a much deeper integration with the organisation's overall value proposition for current and future employees'.

This total re-invention of place has afforded ATI, according to Gillian, 'significant room to breathe, offering freedom, creativity and connection'.

Once the concept of office has moved to the idea of a 'wienie', as a destination, all sorts of possibilities open up. Josephine Kelliher, art curator and implementor of art experiences in corporate settings, highlighted how one global corporation has fully embraced the idea of place as something so much more through the medium of art. Not only did they get behind the idea of artistic thinking as a key development tool, but they also supported the creation of art rooms for various crafts that included painting, pottery, photography and needlework. Office as craft studio tied to real learning outcomes like creativity, empathy, resilience and more highlights how far we can go when it comes to the very idea of a place where work happens. According to Josephine, 'We were able to show quite quickly that 60 minutes away from the desk, in a different space within a space, engaging in an art-based experience, changed employees' mood and mindset significantly'.

Overall, the development of physical spaces will likely become much more holistic, sensory and user centred over the near-term future. Wearing our societal whisperer mindset, how we think about place is definitely becoming more technicoloured. Moving away from ideas of an office as a place mostly for presence and productivity towards a focus on collaboration, creativity, inclusion, spontaneity, wellbeing and ultimately a level of transformation that all great destinations provide. Fields like the areas highlighted below are increasing in sophistication and application and provide multiple avenues for creating places that not only entice, engage and excite but actively improve social, physical and mental wellbeing.

- **Architectural Design Theory:** The exploration of principles and philosophies that guide the design of buildings and spaces, including their psychological impacts.
- **Cognitive Neuroscience:** The study of how brain structures and functions relate to cognitive processes and behaviours.
- **Neuroscience of Space Perception:** Research focused on how the brain interprets spatial information and how this affects our experience of architectural spaces.
- **Environmental Psychology:** The examination of the interplay between individuals and their surroundings, particularly how architecture and design influence human behaviour.

- **Transformational Tourism:** The study and design of deep sensual and emotional transformational experiences that enable people to achieve their full potential as unique and authentic human beings.

By way of illustration let's take one 'small' aspect of place design—colour, which is an area that at least most of us will have had some exposure to (whilst picking colours for a bathroom or bedroom). Colour psychology and its use can be very impactful in terms of influencing mood and motivation. John Hench, continuing our Disney theme, author of *Designing Disney* and an innovator in colour theory, revealed the importance of using colours for training eyes to not notice things (Hench, 2003). If the Disney parks want to hide a metal box containing wiring in a flower bed, they paint it what they call 'Go Away Green'—a muted colour that is completely inoffensive and almost invisible amongst the multi-hued glory of Disney theme parks. The future office place, in essence, needs to be considered as a destination, regardless of the size or scope available to an organisation. The same concepts apply across digital and virtual places. Think more theme park, tourist attraction, event or transformational experience and you are in the right general vicinity.

Questions to help you think

1. What does the workplace mean now to our organisation?
2. What level of experience are you currently providing in the physical space?
3. How well have you integrated different needs into the space?
4. How well have you linked your physical spaces to the overall strategic goals of the organisation?
5. What if you designed the space from an experience-first perspective? What would you change?
6. How inclusive is the design of your spaces and how have you sought out inclusive voices to create something meaningful for everyone?
7. How much are you harnessing the latest thinking in areas like neuro architecture?
8. How might you create a space that acts more like an attractor and excites people?

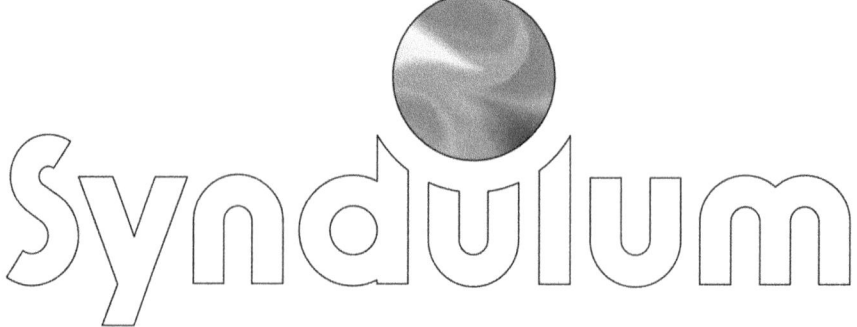

Jump 6: Syndulum—The Company That Fell into the Future

FWW podcast interview with CEO of Syndulum Elisha Harmody, June 2028.

Thanks for taking the time to talk to me Elisha. Great to have you on the FWW podcast.

Great to be here Barry.

You're often and widely quoted that 'Syndulum isn't a bank it's a social enterprise providing financial services and meaningful membership'. Can you explain what you mean by that?

Yes. Syndulum is a social financial enterprise enabled by a community network of connected credit unions to provide a genuine alternative to more traditional financial institutions. Our core idea is to play big but also small—small in the sense we are integral to our local communities' success and big as we play to the multiplication effects of our network and shared capabilities and scale.

Why does Syndulum make sense today?

We believe that due to changing ideas and beliefs about society, the credit union concept is completely modern—even future proof I would say—if we think about the current generation's obsessiveness with social impact, community, meaning and a deeper reason for being. The credit union movement aligns with all of those.

I know one of your bug bears is being compared to retail banks. Let's get into that a bit. What are the differences?

I'm asked a lot about the differences between credit unions and more obvious retail banks. And I always do the same thing. I refer to the seven core principles from the International Co-operative Alliance (ICA) to highlight the significant differences from more traditional business models.

(At this point Elisha refers to a small card taken from her jacket pocket and proceeds to read the seven principles. These are slightly edited but directly from the ICA).

- ***Voluntary and Open Membership:*** *Co-operatives are voluntary organisations, open to all persons able to use their services and willing to accept the responsibilities of membership, without gender, social, racial, political or religious discrimination.*

- ***Democratic Member Control:*** *Co-operatives are democratic organisations controlled by their members, who actively participate in setting their policies and making decisions. Men and women serving as elected representatives are accountable to the membership. In primary co-operatives, members have equal voting rights (one member, one vote) and co-operatives at other levels are also organised in a democratic manner.*

- ***Member Economic Participation:*** *Members contribute equitably to, and democratically control, the capital of their co-operative. At least part of that capital is usually the common property of the co-operative. Members usually receive limited compensation, if any, on capital subscribed as a condition of membership.*

- ***Autonomy and Independence:*** *Co-operatives are autonomous, self-help organisations controlled by their members. If they enter into agreements with other organisations, including governments, or raise capital from external sources, they do so on terms that ensure democratic control by their members and maintain their co-operative autonomy.*

- **Education, Training and Information:** *Co-operatives provide education and training for their members, elected representatives, managers and employees so they can contribute effectively to the development of their co-operatives. They inform the general public—particularly young people and opinion leaders—about the nature and benefits of co-operation.*
- **Co-operation among Co-operatives:** *Co-operatives serve their members most effectively and strengthen the co-operative movement by working together through local, national, regional and international structures.*
- **Concern for Community:** *Co-operatives work for the sustainable development of their communities through policies approved by their members.*

Making the idea of membership real and meaningful has been one of your big goals. How have you been making this happen?

I love the example of one member—a small business owner, John Twamey. As part of our business membership community—Jump—John became part of the SMB business chapter comprised of more than 10,000 business owners. This community also links to the broader CU membership groups, giving access to over 150,000 potential customers and partners. Over the past three years, John's business membership means he has gained access to an accessible marketplace, cheaper consultancy support, real-world insight from other SMB owners and more, helping him scale his business. I spoke to John recently and he puts a lot of his success down to the opportunities that 'membership in action' has given him.

What is important to you going into the future? What are the principles that are going to guide you?

First and foremost, it is to continuously re-enforce our uniqueness as a financial social enterprise. Once we continue to commit to this, it will always keep us focused on the right type of approach for our members, and the right type of services. We will continue growing out our 'member first, digitally savvy' strategy to make sure we are linking magic to membership. Finally, we know we are dealing with an ever-increasing environment of compliance and transparency, and we are committed to using the best intelligent technologies to ensure compliance is built into our processes with minimum time overhead so we can spend more time with our members.

Thanks, Elisha.

No problem, Barry. A pleasure.

6 | Worktask

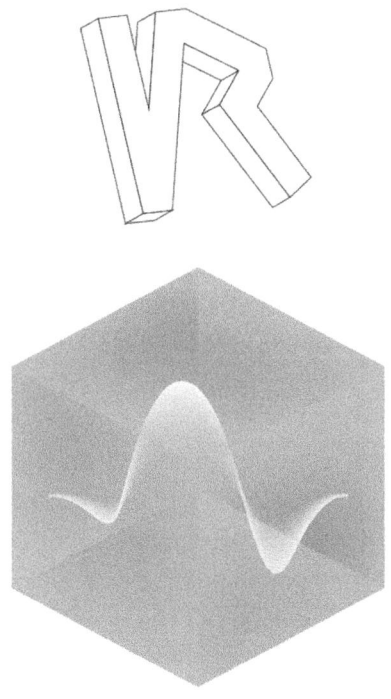

Idealities Realities

I know what you're thinking. Why hasn't the A word been dropped yet? Or more precisely, why haven't the A words been dropped yet in any meaningful way? Automation. Augmentation. Agentic. Artificial. A lot is (or at least mostly) captured in those four words. We could also throw other words into this technological witches' brew—like Industry or Manufacturing 3.0, 4.0, 5.0, X.0—that represent catch-all terms for industries maturing into a dream state of connective technological and digital mastery (with a nod to infinite resilience and authentic human centricity). It can often feel that these words are the only ones spoken or written about when it comes to our future work world. There is a growing tsunami of research, start-ups and gurus on the topic. And rightly so. The AI revolution presents us with probably the biggest disruption to work since, well, since never.

On the one hand we might envisage a utopian dream of a world with no nasty work, universal wages for all and the flowering of a new dawn of creativity and imagination. On the other hand a bleak, almost 'The Matrix'-like existence with unethical practices and an even greater marginalisation of society's most vulnerable. Both extremes are likely to happen in tandem, based on different cultural contexts. But the reality—and this is the reality: no one really knows how all of this will impact society and how we work in totality. Indeed, by the time this book hits the shelves, anything said specifically about the subject by me will seem old hat. It is the very nature of this exponential, self-developing behemoth.

But let's take a breath and go down a level to the practical. From insights extracted via our FOWI network events and discussions, at an organisational level, most of the focus in 2025 (and probably for 2–3 years after that) is centred around building AI understanding and maturity, integrating AI into broader technology strategies, conducting some projects in specific areas, whilst keeping an eye on legislation, compliance and the very secure use and treatment of data. As with all industry disruptions there is the usual mix of laggards, learners, lead innovators and big dream sellers. The structure of most strategic conversations is centred around the different flavours and levels of automation and augmentation, replacement and reshaping that could be harnessed to drive new forms of efficiency, cost savings and innovation.

HR and Talent Acquisition—A Microcosm of Technological Change

Without trying to 'boil the AI ocean', it is worth taking a business function, in this case the HR function, as a microcosm of how AI is impacting and enabling teams across core HR activities. The value of adopting AI in HR functions and associated talent resourcing teams has been well heralded for a while (e.g., Bersin, 2018). However, its level of real adoption seems only now to be picking up momentum as suppliers increase integration of AI into their platforms and solutions, and HR leaders start to pilot AI usage in key functional areas. Celestin and Vanitha (2023) highlight a clear growth in adoption across recruitment, onboarding, performance evaluation and employee engagement, with areas like recruitment and employee engagement growing at a higher rate—58% and 55% adoption, respectively. As of 2025, according to the World Economic Forum (2024), there are over 250 AI tools available for the HR sector.

The case studies of impact are equally growing. Chatbots, a form of conversational AI, and their effectiveness are well documented. A study conducted by Koivunen et al. (2022) found that chatbots were effective, as part of the recruitment process, in improving the candidate experience by providing quick and accurate responses to candidate's queries. Leading organisations like Gartner and McKinsey (Gartner, 2020; McKinsey & Co., 2022) have highlighted the growing role in areas like enhancing employee performance. LinkedIn's *Workplace Learning Report* (2024) has highlighted how L&D professionals are saying that AI helps build skills more effectively.

According to Celestin and Vanitha (2023), AI adoption is linked to a 3% annual decrease in traditional HR roles. A concurrent 8% rise in AI-specific HR jobs highlights role reallocation rather than outright replacement. Reallocation is to new roles like AI ethics consultants, AI-driven data analysts and human–AI interface managers. This research aligns with FOWI research highlighting the short/medium-term impacts as reshaping versus predominantly replacing. As in many professions, it is likely that the AI revolution will shift demand in upskilling and require a shift in mindset, in the case of HR towards strategy, orchestration and innovation.

AI and Deep Human Understanding

A good illustrative example of AI in action in a deeply human context is innovative start-up, and sometime collaborator of the FOWI, Lua Health. One of the biggest challenges in research is the dreaded (my descriptive word) survey. Used a lot by organisations to get a pulse or a vibe of something within an organisation, immediately their use introduces a level of bias. Many would question their validity, especially in the late competitive orange (remember your societal whisperer mindset) era and the strive for awards and commendations. These challenges also extend to other survey assessments around wellness, leadership and other application areas. They can often take a lot of time, can be difficult to get statistically meaningful responses from and analysis can be an imprecise process. Using our systems architect mindset we can say, 'we want all the insight of a survey without a survey'. Previously this would have sounded, in Arthur C. Clarke's words, 'like magic'—but not today. It directed us to an organisation, Lua Health, focused on using AI-driven linguistic inference to get a real, unbiased view of an organisation's attraction health without the need for surveys. In simple terms, an AI-empowered model can derive levels of stress and wellbeing from capturing social sentiment and analysing the type of language used. What excites about this type of technology is its ability to derive serious insight without the need for traditional surveys. Lua's own research and solutions development is very much focused on being able to derive deep insights based on language used via team-based chat platforms to give individuals meaningful insights into their own wellbeing and mental health.

More Than AI—Connecting the Ps

And it's not all about AI. We can't forget about the overall convergence and connectivity of platforms, people and purpose. Often referred to as Industry 4.0 or 5.0. Isaac Care, a highly innovative start-up in the connected homecare space, part of Servisource, led by visionary CEO Declan Murphy, is a great example of utilising a perfect convergence of technology, people and insights. At the core of Issac Care sits the 'Circle of Care' app, a free family caring app which brings all the information gathered from peripheral devices like fall sensors, monitors, watches and more into one place. The app features a client profile, where details about the service user can be shared with a wide group of friends and family members involved in their care; these groups are known as 'circles of care'. Connected devices have been around for a while. What is unique about Isaac Care's approach is the fact that sister organisation Servisource sources, resources and manages the carers that represent the 'people' aspect of the total care approach. Industry 5.0 in action—connected digital and physical platform, human carer and caree centred, and a model that enables people to stay at home longer. A resilient model for future care.

Realising Ideality

For the more astute of you (or those who have read Part I of the book), you should have already gleaned the 'why' of the title of this meta wave. As per our systems architect mindset, AI and enabling technologies are bringing organisations to a place of ideality reality—at least as it pertains to systems efficiency. Whether that be processes, platforms or products. Whatever our ideality vision is, it is likely that AI and other enabling technologies can now get us close to that level of ideality. The magical, dreamlike, unreachable goal of ideality, to paraphrase Altshuller, could quickly become the everyday, the mundane. Figure 17 highlights what the ideality vision could be across selected functions of HR and talent. It offers at once an exciting and a scary prospect. Moving beyond hyper-efficiency into a new form, that of hyper-ideality.

HR Function	Current Reality State	Ideality Vision	AI/Tech Enablers
Recruitment	Digital & Manual screening, interviews, bias	The right candidate finds and selects the right job automatically	AI-matching engines, skills-based hiring platforms, autonomous job agents
Onboarding	Paperwork, orientation sessions	New hires are instantly productive with zero ramp-up	Digital twins, immersive onboarding via AR/VR, AI-guided workflows
Performance Management	Annual reviews, subjective feedback Platform based	Real-time, objective performance insights with self-correcting feedback	Continuous feedback platforms, AI performance analytics
Learning & Development	One-size-fits-all training, some customisation	Employees learn exactly what they need, when they need it, without asking	Adaptive learning systems, AI-curated microlearning
Employee Engagement	Digital surveys, town halls, pulse	The system senses disengagement and resolves it before it happens	Sentiment analysis, predictive engagement models
Workforce Planning	Reactive headcount planning. Low to mid-level sophistication	The system anticipates talent needs and fills gaps proactively	Predictive analytics, AI-driven talent marketplaces
Compliance & Admin	Manual audits, policy enforcement	Compliance is automatic and invisible	Smart contracts, AI policy engines, blockchain records

Figure 17   Ideality realities for HR tasks

What Colour Will Your Ideality Be?

In this age of ideality reality, what coloured glasses will you look through? What core code or mix of codes will you use to guide decision making? In a way, this is the central question. Is the goal when it comes to AI purely an efficiency one—based primarily on orange-code thinking—which early indicators would suggest is the main code of current AI implementation. Or is the goal more green/yellow with an authentic focus on developing massive technological proficiency to reshape workforces sustainably and unleash levels of collaboration, creativity and role reinvention? Can or will organisations make this leap? It might well offer a path more in line with creating destinations for talent versus hyper-ideal organisations with only a courteous, shallow nod to the greater human centricity many of us crave. Implementation of such an exponential technology should not, perhaps, solely be left in the hands of the technologists. It should firstly align with the core philosophy of the firm and what that firm is trying to be from both a people and a societal perspective.

Questions to help you think

1. Where could you apply IFR thinking in your organisation? Where are the places that you can most quickly achieve all the benefits and practically none of the costs and harm?
2. How are you bringing Industry 5.0 to bear across all business units? Beyond the obvious like manufacturing or operations? How are you connecting and converging?
3. What one process could you take and make more ideal in less than 30 days by using an AI-enabled solution?
4. What is your philosophy of the firm as it relates to the age of ideality? Do you have one? What code are you basing your thinking on? Does it encapsulate organisational sustainability from a people perspective? Does it allow for the reinvention and reshaping of people and roles?
5. Have you thought about your business unit in the age of ideality? Have you IFR mapped all of your core processes and activities?
6. How are you using new technologies to increase levels of belonging, sense making and wellbeing for your teams?

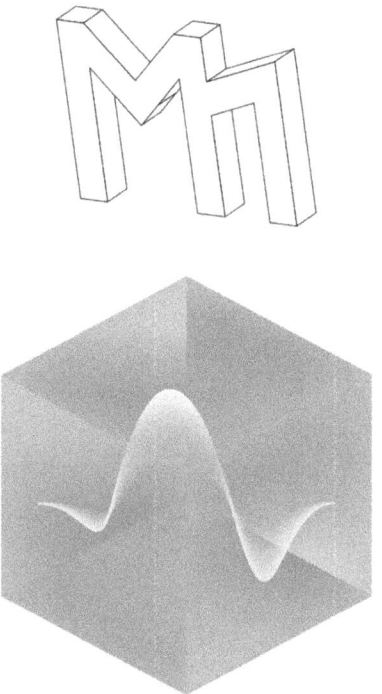

Evolving Sensibilities

One of my all-time favourite bands is Led Zeppelin. The thunderous drumming of John Bonham, the screaming falsetto of Robert Plant, the otherworldly guitar shredding of Jimmy Page and the always refined bass lines of John Paul Jones never ceased to get me into the rock zone. My favourite album of theirs is 'Led Zeppelin IV', which I was first sonically exposed to via my brother-in-law in 1987. What fascinated me about that album, apart from the fantastic songs, was the associated art direction and use of symbols to represent each member of the band. Jimmy's was the ZoSo symbol, resembling the alchemical symbol for Saturn. John P's was a triquetra within a circle, said to symbolise competence. John B's had three interlocking rings symbolising the trinity of mother, father and child. Robert's was a feather enclosed in a circle, representing truth and balance. My impressionable teenage mind went into overdrive and before I knew it, I became obsessed with the meaning of signs and symbolism. Well in advance of the mass future fan obsession of Dan Brown's excellent novels I should say. I was somewhat of an early adopter!

The Circle

If there is one simple icon that symbolically sums up how organisations and indeed leaders need to evolve sensibilities in relation to impact beyond economic value creation, a little like Robert Plant's choice, it is the circle (see Figure 18). In Zen Buddhism, the ensō—a hand-drawn circle—embodies enlightenment, the void and the beauty of imperfection. It also represents inclusivity and equality. Unlike a hierarchy or a line, a circle has no top or bottom, no privileged position. This also makes it a powerful metaphor for community, unity and shared purpose. From a psychological perspective, Carl

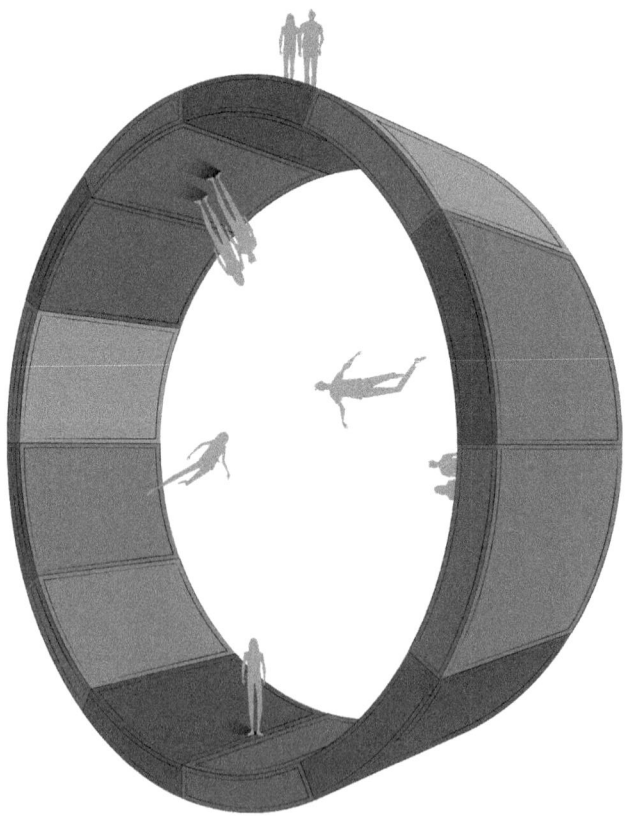

Figure 18   The circle

Jung saw the circle as an archetype of the self—a symbol of psychic wholeness and integration. In dreams and art, circular imagery often appears during times of personal transformation or healing. The process of individuation, in Jungian psychology, is often visualised as a journey towards the centre of a circle—a return to one's true self. In systems thinking, the circle represents feedback loops, interconnectedness and non-linear causality. Unlike linear models, circular systems acknowledge complexity and the dynamic interplay of parts. This is especially relevant in innovation, where circular thinking fosters iteration, learning and adaptation. The rise of the circular economy—a model that emphasises re-use, regeneration and sustainability—also reflects a shift from extractive, linear thinking to holistic, circular design.

Bladebridge—Deeply Circular

Bladebridge, a start-up focused on repurposing decommissioned wind-turbine blades into pedestrian bridges, shelters and other infrastructure, is an example of an organisation that is circular from birth. CEO Angie Nagle's journey to circularity began in the rugged expanse of Alaska, when, as a child, she and her family would haul their rubbish to a local dump. The constant visibility of that dump at the edge of town left a lasting impression on Angie, who realised that 'you don't throw "stuff" away, frankly there is no such thing as "away"'. This early exposure of the material reality of waste would later become the philosophical bedrock of her work, and the core DNA of Bladebridge. After a successful corporate career, she began to experiment with circular business models. The Baby Markets was a grass-roots initiative where parents could buy and sell used baby goods. According to Angie: 'It was a testbed for a bigger idea: could the things we discard be re-imagined into something of value?' Bladebridge, born out of bringing her PhD research into the real world, is based on a deceptively simple concept: take wind-turbine blades destined for landfill and turn them into infrastructure. Execution is anything but simple. Each blade is a complex composite structure and designing with the material, not against it, is at the heart of the business. As Angie puts it, 'letting the object's existing structural and performance characteristics guide the design is a deeply circular concept'.

The company is about much more than a clever engineering solution; it is a statement on how we think, build and live. It is obvious that Angie is just as passionate, if not more so, about the human side of circularity.

Especially in the power of craft and community to improve social challenges. 'There's something healing about working with your hands. I want
to create a business where people don't have to be on the computer all day,
where they can work with their hands, re-imagine what's already there and
feel a deep sense of purpose'.

What is noble about Bladebridge is the true and holistic commitment
to circular as a state of mind, a philosophy of thinking and doing as much as
anything else. As with many circular-based businesses, a key challenge will
be maintaining their core principles as they grow, balancing the push of
corporate-style scaling versus the deep pull of remaining steadfast to their
principles, in a world that is only starting to wake from its linear slumber.

Becoming Responsible

We find ourselves in an age where businesses must become more sustainable in
response to dramatic climate and environmental crises. Legislation like the EU
Green Deal is bringing this new agenda to the boardroom and to the minds of
CFOs, who heretofore never had to wear their sustainability hats. The corporate sustainability reporting directive saw the initial wave of PLCs publish their
first sustainability statements in 2025, initiating the promise of a new dawn for
environmental, governance and sustainability (ESG) disclosure and transparency. A directive that could, in time, drive systemic change. Dr Declan Bogan,
learning director at sustainability pioneer Goodbody Clearstream, highlights
that the current sustainable organisation reality, not unlike the AI reality, is a
mix of maturity levels from laggards to leading lights (like Unilever), who are
setting ambitious targets like net zero, driving their suppliers to, for example,
provide them with directly related carbon footprint data.

From their many projects with leading organisations, Goodbody
Clearstream can see firsthand the positive impact these approaches can have.
The 'return on sustainability investment' can be significant across three pri-
mary areas: strategic value, compliance and risk/operational.

For Goodbody Clearstream, acting sustainably for organisations, practically, means operating in a way that is environmentally, socially and economically sustainable for the long term, with ESG providing a specific set
of criteria for data collection that can be measured and benchmarked
against. This, in turn, provides leadership with the insights they need to

make meaningful decisions. Goodbody Clearstream prefer the term 'responsible business' when it comes to better describing this comprehensive approach to organisational sustainability. A term that has mixed origins—from industrialists like the Cadburys, Carnegies and Tatas who were pioneers in integrating philanthropy and social welfare into their business models and in writings by economist Howard Bowen who published *Social Responsibilities of the Businessman* in 1953, widely regarded as the foundational text of corporate social responsibility (CSR) (Bowen, 1953).

The Rise and Re-Rise of Social

The World Economic Forum suggests that today, there are over 10 million social enterprises putting purpose before profit, tackling pressing issues like climate change and poverty. They account for $2 trillion in annual turnover, creating 200 million jobs. Interestingly, there is no true common definition of what social enterprises are. Some authors seem to focus predominantly on the social-value aspect, ignoring economic outcomes, while others associate economic value with these types of organisations despite it not being the primary goal. Kerlin Monroe-White (2016) argue against a common definition due to significant differences in factors like form of government, culture, model of civil society and stages of economic development. The European Commission's definition is probably the most useful for our purposes: 'an operator in the social economy whose main objective is to have social impact rather than make a profit for their owners or shareholders'. The combination of having a meaningful social impact coupled with the need for sustainable economic revenue makes social enterprises unique and differentiates them from other organisational forms (like non-profits).

From research like that of Chatzopoulou and de Kiewiet (2021), Rank (2021), Narayanan (2022) and Sawicka (2023), it seems that younger generations, including Millennials and Gen Zs, feel more favourably towards brands that authentically prioritise social values, environmental concerns and sustainability, and prefer companies that contribute positively to society and the environment. From a FOWI perspective, we know that meaningful societal initiatives and environmental sensitivity are becoming more important in relation to an organisation's overall employer value proposition and how that proposition attracts potential employees.

From Here to There or from There to Here?

It isn't too far of a stretch to say that all organisations (and the leaders leading them) must become more social, more sustainable, more sensitive to their total impact and how they create current and future value. Evolving their business sensibilities with a deeply circular philosophy at the core. As technological sophistication increases, it may well be that an evolved sensibility becomes the key differentiator in attracting and retaining employees and customers alike. With our societal whisperer mindset, we know that there are significant opportunities in becoming more deeply green and taking if not giant strides into a yellow/turquoise-code future, then at least a few educated and tentative steps. In a corporate world that has been predominantly blue/orange in code for such a long time (and in many ways still is), organisational models like collectives and co-operatives are often viewed as less efficient, less technological and less professionally run. Less desirable.

But the flow of the wave is very much towards these types of business models. Or, to be more precise, business models that are inherently more green/yellow. The success of organisations like Mondragon shows that it is possible to have a core code that is deeply green with aspects of orange, yellow and turquoise. At FOWI we have worked with these types of collective-based businesses. There is a growing realisation, at least with some of the co-operative leaders we work with as part of a future foresight engagement, that these types of models may perhaps represent a more sophisticated and sensitive future. Something different. But even those leaders appreciate that they are not truly maximising the social value and impact that these types of organisations have and can have into the future. In a previous life, one of my responsibilities was a yearly trust survey, which benchmarked key pillars of trust with customers against other competitors. One competitor grouping were co-operatives and, regardless of the relative sophistication of my own organisation at the time, trust in those organisations with customers was always significantly higher. This aligns with research on the topic comparing trust in collectives versus corporate organisations. Gerhard Kosinowski (2020), in a chapter from *Responsible Business in a Changing World*, highlights how co-operatives are inherently community oriented, and this orientation is not an add-on (as in CSR for corporations) but embedded in their DNA. This embeddedness leads to greater stakeholder trust, especially in financial cooperatives, where members feel a stronger sense of ownership and accountability.

It is likely that all organisations will have to become more deeply societal, more circular, more sensitive to being sustainable entities into the future. Fully integrating these practices from top to bottom so that they become 'the way of doing things' as opposed to legally enforced, disconnected practices. And for those organisations like collectives, co-operatives and social enterprises, the opportunity is to fully embrace and harness their future-facing 'different'. Leaders will need to take inspiration from the symbol of the circle and the entirety of what that means to be the leaders that their colleagues, communities and societies need.

Questions to help you think

1. How circular is your thinking?
2. Is a line or a circle a more appropriate representation of your organisation?
3. What does responsible business mean to your business?
4. Have you created your own core sustainability themes that make sense for the business you are in, beyond the legal requirements?
5. How well integrated—across, up and down—is your approach to being responsible?
6. What might happen if you thought more like a social enterprise, a collective or a co-operative in how you ran your business?
7. How would you design your next process if it was fully circular?
8. What are you doing to link these types of practices with your overall employer value proposition and employee experience?
9. How would your approach to business change if you thought more in terms of green/yellow codes?
10. How well developed is your thinking on how these approaches will create new opportunities for real value creation?

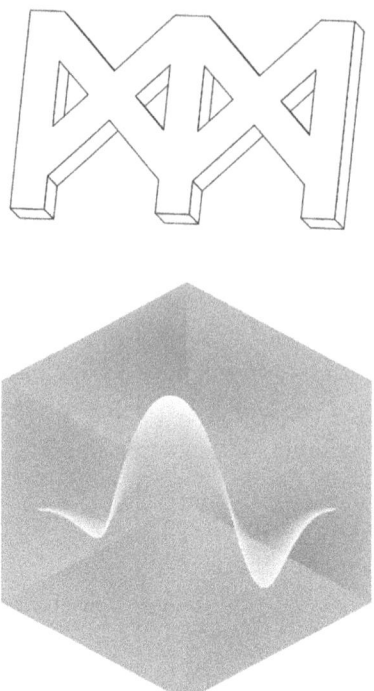

Mixed Ms

When it comes to getting work done in a democratic and empowering way, we can learn a lot from the Fab Five. No, you didn't read that wrong. It's not the usual Fab Four lads from Liverpool I am referring to, but five seriously fashion-conscious musicians from Birmingham.

Drummer Roger Taylor once said about Duran Duran (who became known as the Fab Five in the 1980s): 'It's totally democratic. . . that's one of the big things. That every decision must be run through the whole band. You don't have one person that makes any decision on their own'. In an interview with Channel 4 News in 2023, Simon LeBon (the lead singer and primary lyricist) highlighted that they were 'willing to sacrifice our egos for the good of the band'. It's very well known that the band split income equally across all members.

Across multiple interviews, band members have highlighted how important this democratic approach has been in the band's longevity. In an interview from 2015 on duranduran.com, Roger Taylor goes a little deeper on the democratic approach: 'We call the band "the group conscience", that's the four of us and that's very strong. We are able to let people in with confidence knowing it's not going to disrupt the balance of the band. I don't think we could have done that a few years ago. Our egos may have been a little too fragile to let people in'.

In a way, Duran Duran's core philosophies that have kept them together for more than forty years are mirrored in the new world of work. Democracy, collectivism, empowerment, ownership—these concepts are representative of how getting things done and delivering value in organisations is evolving. Methodologies that integrate all these concepts—like self-managed teams and indeed self-managed organisations—have been around for a while, with a small number of highly acclaimed examples like Buurtzorg, Orpheus and Spotify. And they have been extensively researched. But they have yet to take full hold at a strategic, organisation or team level. In fact, the norm from our experience at the FOWI seems to be a limited number of small, isolated islands of self-managing teams, often surrounded by a sea of more traditional top-down organisation structures. Morikawa et al. (2024) bring an interesting aspect to bear when it comes to self-managing systems. They differentiate between two types: organisation-level structural decentralisation and employee-level decision rights. Or put simply, Big S and Little S. One is focused on formal decentralisation of authority throughout the organisation and the other centres on the level of employee rights across execution, direction setting and organisational development. It could be argued that the Little S is easier to get at, more accessible for organisations dipping their toes into the future of work.

Like all approaches, whether it's Big S or Little S, we know from wearing our systems mindset that each new system presents new challenges as people need to learn new languages, new tools and novel approaches. As a result making the leap to another system can be tricky. However, flow would suggest that getting work done is moving towards an increasing level of empowerment to those delivering the work. Especially in a world where the seismic impact of AI is driving a re-assessment of delivering work tasks and an increasing meta working world that has changed notions of place and presence.

Getting Close to Self

The rise, for example, of human-centred, methodologically empowered approaches like Agile, and associated methods like Scrum, point towards a pragmatic 'third way' that, when done properly, removes some of the challenges of traditional delivery approaches and prioritises greater ownership of the work itself and often a greater sense of empowerment. In a way, getting closer to the ideals of self-management. In a comparative analysis study conducted by Ogirri and Idugie (2024), use of agile approaches resulted in a 21% higher rate of project success compared to more traditional PM (project management) methods. Projects using agile exhibited a 20% increase in customer satisfaction as per NPS (net promoter scores). The study also highlighted that team members engaged in various agile projects reported higher levels of empowerment, motivation and better work–life balance compared to traditional projects. An interesting piece of work by Koch and Schermuly (2020) suggests that agile PM can attract individuals who seek novel, complex and intense sensations. They suggest that, in the right contexts, organisations should highlight their practice of empowering, agile PM methodologies and practices as part of their employer brand to attract future specialists for agile projects.

James Louttit, author of *Leading Impactful Teams* (Louttit, 2024) and thought leader in agile and design-led approaches to achieving outcomes, suggests that in this emerging world of work, 'we are all project managers, in way. Life itself is a project'. He notes that whilst methodologies like Scrum and Kanban are extremely useful, they don't necessarily empower teams on their own and as such he advocates for harnessing more human-centred skills like facilitation, empathy, psychology and design thinking in creating sustainable impact. What is interesting is the emphasis he also places on prioritisation—memorably quoting lyrics from 'The Bare Necessities'[1]—focusing on what matters most to connect impact to effort, ultimately driving success and a greater sense of employee empowerment. He also strongly advocates for being flexible in the types of methods used to deliver outcomes, and to focus on the most appropriate 'toolkit' for the challenges at hand.

Getting Sh&T Done Generationally

A growing body of research is highlighting how younger generations like Gen Z are reluctant to work within traditional hierarchical structures. Suanto and Marezza (2025) found that Gen Zs prioritise collaborative decision making, purpose-driven work and work–life integration over traditional power structures. Pantelides (2025) further highlights that Gen Zs favour a distinct democratic approach to working life, with leaders that exhibit democratic or even a laissez faire style of leadership. Whilst the preferences of this younger generation are critical to designing models of work delivery that, well, work, it is important to recognise the current multi-generational aspect of today's workforce. This adds an extra layer of challenge for leaders and indeed teams in attempting to get things done. Baby Boomer managers tend to favour direct communication and command and control approaches, while Millennials favour constructive, collegiate feedback. Whilst many studies highlight differences between generations in how they lead and want to be led, I would suggest that there is a growing green and yellow code hue across all generations and that the expectations are definitely moving towards an empowered, democratic and collaborative approach to getting things done.

I'm with the Band

At FOWI, we are very much committed to the core ideas of getting things done in an empowering, 'like self' way. As you might have guessed by now, given the number of music analogies and stories scattered throughout this book, the FOWI team are into their music (with highly diverse tastes from metal to mellow). We use the analogy of 'the band' (see Figure 19) as our way of getting things done. In alignment with the concepts of self-managing teams we live by a set of principles, more like explicit assumptions, which guide our work.

This approach lends itself to an elevated level of empowerment, as well as sustaining a key focus on creativity and client focus, which is essential in the work that we do. Team meetings are kept to a minimum, and the leadership approach is highly collaborative, with predominantly a coaching style of leadership. This can lead to certain levels of confusion but the positive impact in terms of ownership over projects, feelings of accomplishment and the significant amount of successful innovation projects and research far outweigh the challenges. In a high-trust environment, confusion can be dealt with rapidly.

Metahuman Magic

'Metahuman' was a term first coined by DC Comics in the 1980s. It refers to individuals who possess abilities beyond the normal human range. Beings who

Figure 19   FOWI band principles

transcend human limitations and harness exciting powers and abilities. Marvel uses 'mutants' or 'enhanced individuals' to get across a similar general concept. Think Superman or Spiderman. My favourite character in the realms of super-herodom technically isn't a 'metahuman' in the narrow sense of the word. But I'd argue that Iron Man, thanks to his use of sophisticated technology and early use of AI (to ensure his heroic legacy would outlast him, Tony Stark pro-grammed an AI with his mind and personality),[2] becomes metahuman any-time he suits up. And in a way, the advent of AI technologies and the age of ideality are enabling us to, if not become metahuman, then at least act and do in a more metahuman type of way. These technologies are evolving rapidly, moving towards technological ideality, and the emergence of autonomous AI agents represents the next transformational leap in the AI 'system'. These intelligent systems can make decisions, learn from experiences and execute complex actions with limited or no human involvement. Negnevitsky (2025) best sums it up when he highlights that autonomous AI agents are not merely tools—they are collaborators in a new era of intelligent automation. With these types of enabling technologies, humans can indeed become more like metahumans, delivering levels of work that are unimaginable right now. And, just possibly, begin to see AI agents as the most useful, efficient and creative teammates they have worked with.

The Moves

With a reasonable level of certainty, we can say that getting stuff done, completing work tasks, delivering outcomes—whatever we want to call it—needs to continue its evolution to keep people interested and engaged in what they do, and to attract the talent needed to grow. The following moves offer guidance on the right direction of travel.

- **Rigid to Flexible:** Moving from a fixed mindset and a rigid adherence to a certain way of doing things to a more flexible, adaptable approach.
- **Mono Tool to Poly Tool:** Moving from using a limited toolkit to using a toolkit of multiple methodologies (and technologies) appropriate to changing contexts and challenges.
- **Directed to Self-Directed:** Moving from top-down, directed work to self-directed, collaborative work. From one leader to all leaders based on situation and tasks.
- **People + Tool to People + Agents:** Moving from a narrow view of enabling technologies to one of harnessing the full suite of platforms, tools and intelligent, autonomous technologies that function as collaborator, co-worker and colleague.
- **Method to Meaning:** Moving from method-heavy approaches to a human-centred one, prioritising meaning and purpose. Prioritising human skills like motivational psychology, coaching and facilitation to create strong levels of engagement and association.
- **Broad Values to Practical Assumptions:** Moving from broad-based values to assumptions that actively guide and empower people to work in a more self-managed way.

Questions to help you think

1. How can you bring a little more 'self' to your organisation, business division or team?

2. What might be your perfect mix of methods to give people a greater feeling of empowerment?

3. Do you have a toolkit for getting things done? Is it adequate?

4. What might your explicit assumptions be to guide a more empowered style of work? Practical, explicit assumptions beyond broad values.

5. What would be your first AI agent? What would its job be?

6. How might you harness younger generations in your organisation to create new ways of working and getting things done?

7. What human-centred skills do your teams have or lack to enable a more 'self' way of working?

8. How sensitive are your leaders to generational norms, and other layers of inclusivity, to design customised ways of working?

9. How can you create metahumans in your organisation? What AI superpowers could you provide?

Jump 7: Ludge

Top 10 in the Future Fit 100: Gold Medal Winner 2029.

Summary of Ludge in the Future Fit awards brochure.

Ludge is quickly becoming the most common learning and validation hub for employees. A 'one stop skills shop' for all formal and informal qualifications, badges, project achievements and more. It utilises AI to infer skillsets and constantly understand the evolving skills needed for an employee's current role. It prepares hyper personalised micro and nano learning programmes to keep individuals fully skilled and savvy for the world of work.

One of the most interesting aspects of Ludge is the focus on real-time testing across multiple digital and virtual environments to assess 'levels of mastery'—a first-of-its-kind, scalable approach to true skills validation. What's unique is its use of various forms of unexpected testing approaches—from utilising real-time role play with an avatar to test human skills, to online, real-time virtual group challenges to assess group problem-solving ability. Ludge is winning in an evolving talent market seeking fun, engaging and immersive solutions to personal development.

This third part introduces a usable mixing desk for creating your future work world 'mixes'. Across the 3 Ws and 16 associated equalisers, you will be able to set your current mix and dial the equalisers up and down to imagine possible future work worlds for your organisation. Descriptions are given for each equaliser, and their respective dial-up and dial-down positions. Strategies for breakthrough thinking whilst using the mixing desk are included. Also highlighted are ways to deploy the mixing desk in team and group settings, and facilitation notes to help you on your journey into the future. Supporting templates are also provided in the Appendix at the back of the book. Happy mixing—you are now (unofficially) a future work world producer!

7 | The 3W Mix Desk

Introduction

When I was growing up, all my family were mad about music. To say I was exposed to loud sonic waves in the womb would be an understatement. Both of my parents were powerful singers, and music was everywhere at home. One relative, whilst not a singer or a performer, counted himself a 'listening connoisseur' (his words not mine). He had what he called a 'music room'—a magical place with, at its heart, a state-of-the-art (at the time) combo mixing desk and hi-fi set with a serious number of buttons and a plethora of what were called equalisers (for those younglings out there, do your research—this was the 1980s).

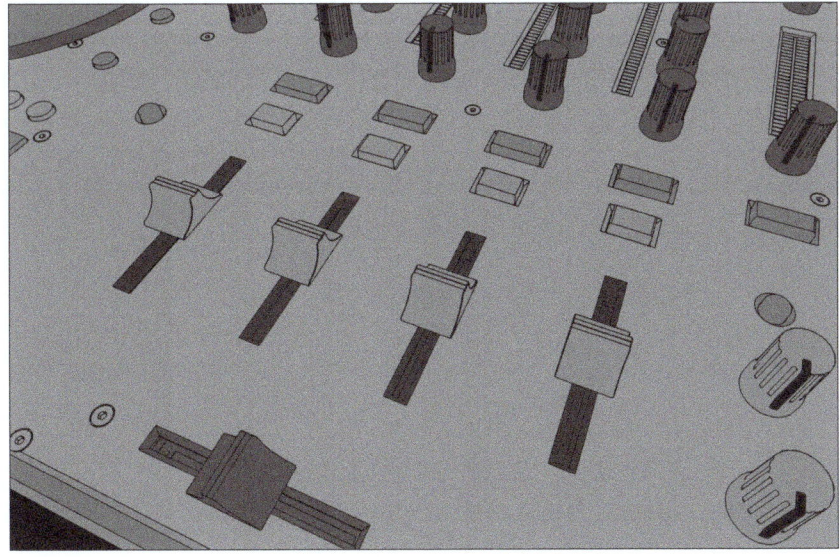

Beside the stereo/mixing desk combo was a document highlighting the optimal settings for each style of music. Classical had a specific configuration of the slider equalisers, funk had a different configuration, and so on. This enabled him to listen to any of his selection of over a thousand LPs in absolute audio perfection. I would often run into the room and mess with his buttons—this would drive him up the wall but provided me with hours of fun, particularly over high days and holidays.

What, pray tell, has all of this got to do with designing your future work world I hear you say? Lots. Just like my relative's old mixing desk, imagine you have a 'future of work' mixing desk set, with equalisers that you can dial up or down. A mixing desk that can be played with, experimented on and used to land on a perfect organisational 'mix'. Welcome to your mixing desk for the future of work. Welcome to the 3W Mix Desk.

You have already been exposed to the three Ws as part of our travels through the systems architect mindset and the nine metawaves. It's now time to harness the next level of depth of these Ws in mapping, imagining and designing your future work world. You should find the 3W Mix Desk comprehensive. It should have just the right number of nobs to play with! It's best NOT to think about the 3W Mix Desk as a maturity or capability model. Hence the use of the phrase 'Mix Desk'. More it is a place to play, to design and produce your own future work world mixes—some of which might go into full design execution, some of which may never see the light of day. Most of all the 3W Mix Desk is about driving strategic imagination (dreaming) and innovation (doing) when it comes to your world of work, helping you to create a destination that will entice, excite and engage. The 3W Mix Desk has been utilised across a number of organisations to date and came out of my work with the Future of Work Institute (FOWI) in 2021–2024; it has been consistently 'tweaked' since then. Is it perfect? No. Is it relevant, impactful and useful? Yes.

Mix Desk Overview

The 3W Mix Desk, as its name implies, is made up of three interconnected Ws. As in our previous chapters, these three Ws are:

- Workplace—the physical, digital and virtual places where work takes place.

- Workforce—the propositions, structures, models and skills that define work.
- Worktask—the mindsets, methods and tools that deliver the work.

Each of these Ws have several equalisers associated with them. There are 16 equalisers in all. Each equaliser captures an important element of the future of work that can be dialled up or down to drive impact. Some of these might be less important to you now but may become more important to you in the future. Left or right on the equalisers does not necessarily mean 'better' or 'worse'—hence the use of the word equalisers. They can be dialled up or dialled down as required based on that 'mix perfection' you are trying to achieve, depending on the factors you want to impact. In general terms, moving the equalisers to the right can be seen as more 'in flow' with some of the metawaves of the future of work.

Figure 20 is an example of the three equalisers associated with workplace. The three equalisers are 'multiverse', 'experiential' and 'presence'. Each equaliser has a left setting and a right setting. You get the idea!

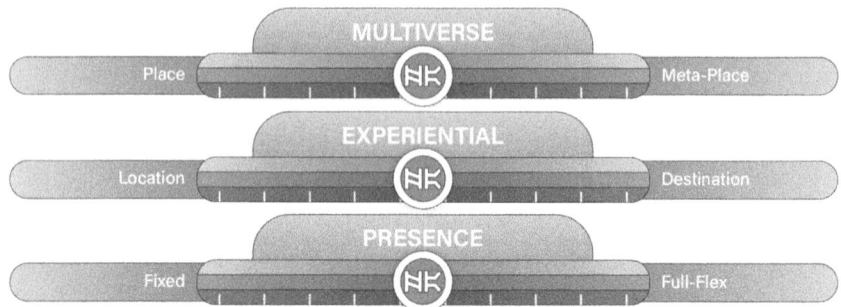

Figure 20   The three equalisers of workplace

Actual application of the 3W Mix Desk is explored in much greater detail in the next chapter, but to give a little application context it can be (and has been) used in multiple ways including:

- Mapping an organisation's current 'as is future work world' mix.
- Exploring a broader set of future of work strategic opportunities.
- 'Swooshing around' in 'could be' futures and options about 'tomorrow'.
- Investigating the value impact of dialling up and dialling down the equalisers.
- Structuring facilitation and awayday sessions related to the future of work, HR, talent and more.
- Connecting the dots across the various equalisers and how they might interact in the near future.
- Brainstorming workplace, workforce and worktask concepts and pinpointing potential innovation pathways.
- 'Going up a level' and improving strategic thinking around the world of work.
- Breaking through narrow thinking about work
- Re-thinking or re-scoping existing initiatives or programmes.
- Better integrating disconnected projects into more of a strategic whole.

As you should well know at this stage, thanks to your focused reading of Part I of the book (!), the use of the mixing desk is only as effective as the depth of thinking you apply whilst using it. Across the following chapters I have attempted to interlace the three mindsets as simply as possible throughout the model application but just as culture eats strategy for breakfast, so too does mindset eat model (or mixing desk) for lunch. So, remember your mindsets, the metawaves and the 'jumps', as you use the mixing desk and apply liberally!

Did You Know. . .

According to *Guinness World Records*, 'Yesterday' has the most cover versions of any song ever written. The song remains popular today, with more than 1600 recorded cover versions. Broadcast Music Incorporated (BMI) asserts that it was performed over seven million times in the 20th century alone. There are many versions of the song—from soul to jazz, even arias and bluegrass versions. All very different. The best of them in my opinion is the one by Marvin Gaye on his 1970 *That's the Way Love Is* album—very smooth. Cathy Berberian, the opera singer, released an entire album of Beatles songs as arias in 1967 that included 'Yesterday'. If that wasn't surreal enough, the cover art for that album was drawn by Gerald Scarfe, who famously did the illustrations for Pink Floyd's *The Wall*. This can be, to some, a useful analogy to think about your 3W Mix Desk sounds—we may be using the same core elements but your version of the future of work mix will be unique to your own context. The 'sound' will be very much your own. In fact, all the organisations we have applied the model in have had very different current and future 'versions' and imaginings.

Introducing the Equalisers

The following sections provide definitions of each of the 16 equalisers across workforce, workplace and worktask. This includes what dialling more to the left or more to the right means. Associated tables are provided in the Appendix at the back of the book.

Workforce

Value

The value—both monetary and non-monetary—that employers provide to their employees and broader workforce (temps, contractors, etc.)

Dialling more to the left means more of a focus on a basic package, generic across most employees. Dialling more to the right means a more fully designed, connected employer value proposition focused on multiple elements, designed and customised with different types of employees in mind, fully integrated into the business, aligned with internal employee engagement and brand and external employer marketing and brand strategies.

Career

The functional, emotional and social journeys that candidates and employees go on throughout their entire careers

Dialling more to the left means several point interventions or initiatives across some parts of the talent journey. Dialling more to the right means greater focus on fully designed, purposeful and experiential talent journeys from pool, interest to attraction, recruitment and retention across different worker types.

Blend

The level and mix of diverse workforce models being used strategically for value creation

Dialling more to the left means a greater focus and preference towards permanent work types with a limited mix. Dialling more to the right means strategically harnessing a mix of employment types across permanent, contractors, suppliers, consultants, partners, SOW (statement of work), gig, pay-by-the-hour workers, fractional leaders to tap into new skills, diversity, innovation and more.

Belonging

The integration of diversity and inclusiveness practices across thinking and doing

Dialling to the left means several point interventions and programmes in relation to legal aspects of diversity. Dialling more to the right means the full integration of the multiple layers of diversity and inclusive thinking/design across leadership, employee and team engagement, strategies, products, services, experiences, projects, operations and brands linked to key business outcomes and indicators.

Structure

The levels of bureaucracy at an organisational level

Dialling more to the left means more of a traditional structural model. Referred to most frequently as hierarchical. Or a variation of hierarchy, like 'The Matrix'. Dialling more to the right means more formal decentralisation of decision-making authority across the organisation. A focus on flatter structures with fewer levels.

Learning

The approaches taken to learning and development

Dialling more to the left means a focus on blended learning and development. Formal structures and learning paths. Some level of customisation. Dialling more to the right means full integration of multi-modal, experiential, personalised, on-demand learning and development across all learning channels. Rich media and trans media. Fully utilising enabling technologies like VR/AR and AI.

Skills

The skills-first orientation of an organisation

Dialling more to the left means a focus on more traditional role-based approaches and role-based design and delivery. Dialling more to the right means a move away from job titles, hierarchies and credentials. Towards skills-based talent practices across hiring, mobility, development and performance. Supported by strong skills intelligence and a more dynamic approach to work design linking macro, micro and nano projects with skills. Skills realms not job roles.

Workplace

Multiverse

The degree of merging of physical, digital and virtual places

Dialling more to the left means use of physical place in combination with elements of digital place. Dialling more to the right means a merging of physical, digital and virtual places, optimising each for different types of work tasks (designing, engaging, learning, delivering) and utilising the unique functionalities and opportunities that each place affords.

Experiential

The extent to which place has been designed from an experience-first perspective

Dialling more to the left means that place has been designed from a functional perspective. Mostly utilitarian with some elements of useful design. Dialling more to the right means having a more experiential workplace across physical, digital and virtual realms focused on the user and their different needs linked to the values, goals and essence of the organisation. Focused on the psychological, emotional and sensory design to engage and empower.

Presence

The overall level of flexibility in terms of location, proximity and presence

Dialling more to the left means a limited level of flexibility in terms of location of work. Work is predominantly conducted in core physical locations or spoke/satellite locations. Some home/third place. Presence is linked to physicality. Dialling to the right means 'flexibility first' and fully integrated. A big focus on all forms of flexible working and practices. Presence not linked mainly to physicality. Remote-working practices might be the primary or only way of working. Work can be delivered equally from any place using sophisticated technologies. All supporting elements are optimised for flexibility.

Worktask

Mindset

The breadth and depth of thinking in leading, designing and delivering

Dialling more to the left means adopting a mindset that is likely unconsciously partial and biased. Dialling more to the right means purposefully adopting a mindset that integrates human, societal and technological thinking and skills across leading people, designing anything and how work gets delivered. From greyscale to technicolour.

Insight

The reach and richness of data and insights to make informed decisions

Dialling to the left means a more reactive, disjointed approach to insights used to support decision making. Dialling more to the right means having a proactive, real-time and predictive pulse across people, processes, products and planet based on qual and quant data.

Methods

The models and methods used to deliver work, value and outcomes

Dialling more to the left means a focus on a limited number of fixed methods and models. Dialling more to the right means utilising a mixed toolbox appropriate to various contexts, colleagues and challenges. More focus on enabling agile thinking and doing. Integration of human-centred models and methods (e.g., design, psychology, anthropology).

Human Machine

The integration of autonomous technologies across organisational tasks

Dialling more to the left means a use primarily of human–machine augmentation and some autonomous activities across a selection of tasks. Dialling more to the right means fully harnessing autonomous task completion using AI autonomous technologies across the full spectrum of strategic, tactical, operational and personal tasks and reshaping the human role in that context.

Empowerment

The scope of personal empowerment and self-direction delegated to teams and team members

Dialling more to the left means a more traditional leader-directed team model with few levels of team empowerment. Dialling more to the right means greater team autonomy over targets and goal setting, team strategy and direction setting, skills development and how work is resourced and delivered by the team.

Value Chain

The level of responsible and circular practices integrated across the organisational value chain

Dialling more to the left means a primarily efficiency/cost/quality approach whilst fulfilling minimum legal requirements relating to sustainability practices fulfilled. Dialling more to the right means adopting primarily a circular, integrated responsible business approach using these practices as critical jumping-off points for innovation and transformation.

8

Time to Mix: What's Our Current Mix?

Introduction

Now that you are fully up to speed on the 3Ws Mix Desk and the 16 equalisers, it's time to start mixing. Time to get your hands slightly sweaty. Let's start with the base mix and set the equalisers based on your current reality.

Starting Out: On Your Own or with a Group?

There are many ways to get to your base, current reality. In my view there are no right or wrong ways. At the Future of Work Institute (FOWI) we have used many approaches. You can start by going at it solo (which I would recommend to get your head around the model prior to broader use), or you can utilise it with a group. The following are a couple of important points to consider prior to using.

- **Be Clear on the Application:** What are you mapping the 'as is' of? Is it the entire organisation, is it a business unit, is it a geographical entity? Is it your own function? You might also be mapping for a 'who' with generational or other psychographic criteria. Either way, be clear on this prior to starting.

157

- **Build Diversity in From the Start if You Can:** Where possible, use a cross-section of views that represent the broadest diversity of voices that you can. This helps to get to a fairly agreeable 'consensus view'.
- **80% is Good Enough:** Don't look for perfection, look for an 80%—where the equalisers positioning is 'just right'—too much time can be spent polishing with no value.
- **Use Evidence or Data Points up to a Point:** When plotting each equaliser, truly ask yourself: 'Are there three points of data that support the positioning?' If there are, then it's more right than wrong. Move to the next equaliser.
- **Avoid Positivity Bias:** From experience, many place the current equaliser settings too high. Spend the time to be objective and, if you can't find evidence points, place the dial lower.

Tables and Templates

Tables and templates can be found in the Appendix at the back of the book. Each of the 3W tables in the Appendix highlights the definition of each equaliser, what dialling to the left and right means for each, and the two 'extreme' positionings of each equaliser. The templates are a visual tool you can use to plot each equaliser in sessions (or on our own). These templates are at the core of creating your future work world current and future mix.

Suggested Approach to Map the 'As Is' (But Use Your Own)

Highlighted below is a tried and tested approach to using the 3W Mix Desk. It is for a group setting. It should work for you. If it doesn't, don't blame the author (!), and find something that works for you.

Setup
- *Start with a small, trusted group (max 15)*

  My experience is that the use of the Mix Desk (in an organisation) is initially introduced via the people function or a leadership team to adopt a more strategic approach to designing the future of work in the business. If this is your situation, then keep the work within the initiating group. Small numbers at this point work well, where the focus is getting to a broad consensus view through meaningful and focused dialogue.

■ *Have at least two groups working on the Mix Desk*

Two groups (or more) ensures that positivity—or indeed negativity—bias is taken out as much as possible. It also promotes 360° conversations on each of the equalisers and drives an evidence-based approach to 'defending' the positioning of each equaliser.

■ *Divide and conquer, or conquer then divide*

It may be useful to ask each participant to complete their own view on each equaliser and then share their results via one of the many questionnaire platforms out there. This gives probably the most honest view but can be problematic if the views diverge massively. But this offers an opportunity to deep dive on the level of divergence. Equally useful is to conduct the initial review as a group and then ask individuals to reflect on the positioning and revert with contrarian views (as long as they are supported by some evidence or data points).

Suggested Flow

■ *Introduce the Mix Desk and the 3Ws/16 equalisers*

The introduction to the Mix Desk is important. Introduce the definition of the future of work as per Chapter 1 at the start of the session. If you have a longer session, introduce an overview of the mindsets. Highlight how the future of work represents a strategic opportunity for the business but it's important to connect the dots on where the business is and what it could/needs to become. Then introduce the overall Mix Desk and the equalisers in a little more detail as provided by the templates.

■ *Start with one W and focus on the 'evidence'*

Take one of the Ws—any one is fine. Distribute the equaliser template to each of the groups you have. Introduce the definition of each equaliser and the two 'extremes'. Focus the conversation on 'are we more like this side of the equaliser or the other?', then move to placing where you believe you currently are. To do this effectively, use the phrase 'we are here because. . .' and use the rule of three (i.e., you as a group need to pinpoint three things that support your 'As Is' position). Conversely (to avoid bias) you may also discuss three things that may bring into question the positioning—or why something should be more dialled up or down based on reality. It can be useful here to think about initiatives or projects that have got you to that position or will shift that position in the future. Ensure you cover all three Ws and the associated 16 equalisers.

Example of an 'As Is' Mix

Figure 21 shows an example of a finalised 'As Is' mix on the equalisers associated. This indicates where you should get to after covering all three Ws. Depending on your organisation, some of these equalisers may be new to you, and you will very likely have mixed levels of dial left and dial right. You may not even think some of the equalisers are relevant but trust me, they are or will be. The point is to provide you with a strategic and holistic model that broadens and deepens your perspective. It is also worth noting that none of the organisations we have worked with had the same Mix Desk settings, and all organisations have different levels of challenge and opportunity across the 3Ws.

What Have the Romans (I Mean, the Position) Ever Done for Us?

Now that you have your base mix, it's time to map the current impact of each equaliser positioning, otherwise known as 'What has this positioning ever done for us?'. This is where the impact value matrix comes in. And this is where you need to think about the relative importance of some of these value creators to your business now and into the future. There is a template in the Appendix at the back of the book to use as part of this process. The value impact matrix covers the impact criteria shown in Figure 22. We are not accountants during this process, but we are interested in the broad strategic impact to the organisation. From experience, it is best to keep this simple. For each position, highlight if it's a current positive, neutral or negative impact on each of the value aspects you are covering. If you want to go further, you can expand to 'highly positive' and 'highly negative' on either side of the three views.

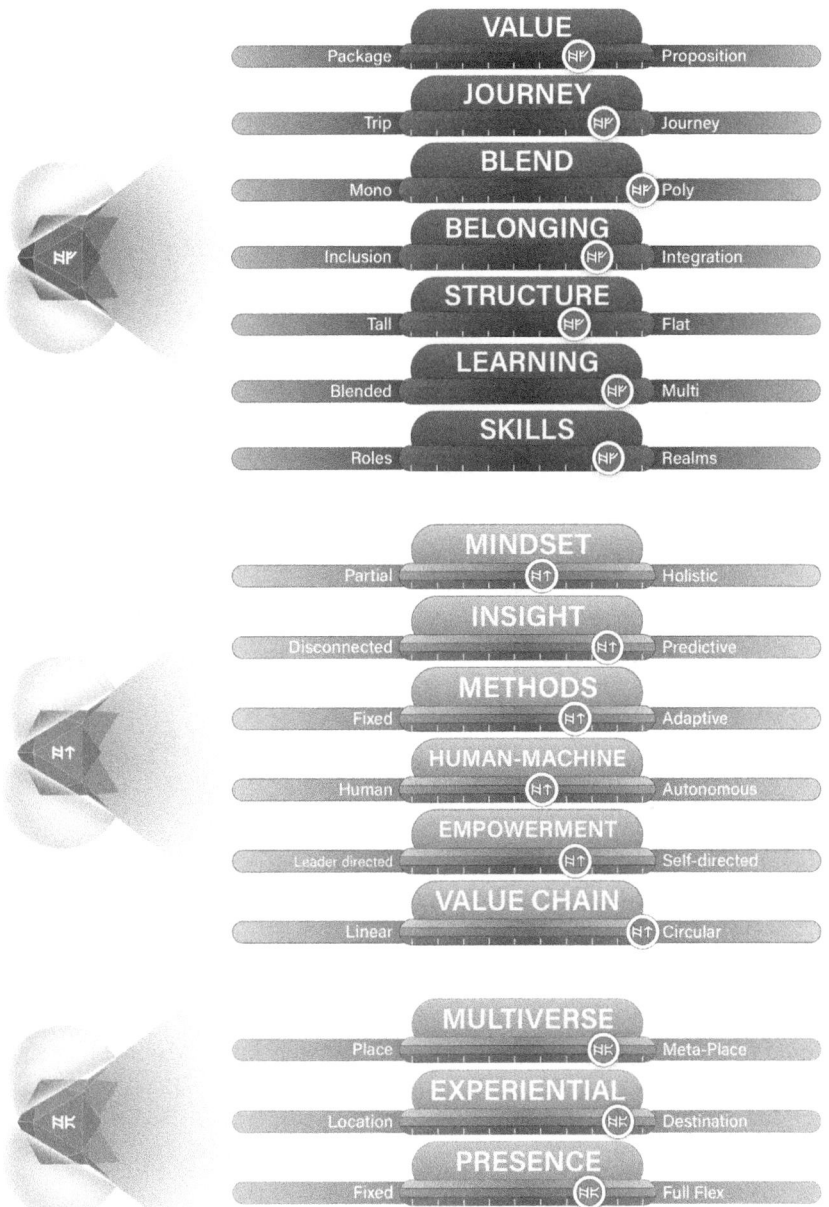

Figure 21   Example of an 'As Is' mix

Attraction	how the positioning helps attract the people needed to deliver our service and success
Retention	how the positioning supports our ability to retain people needed to deliver our service & success
Diversity	how the positioning enables the mix (how we define the mix) of people in our business across multiple aspects of diversity
Sustainability	how the position supports sustainable practices and impacts in our business
Efficiency	how the current position enables efficient work practices, processes and minimises waste
Belonging	how the current positioning supports a sense of ownership, belonging and connection
Innovation	how the current positioning supports new ideas & different thinking
Wellbeing	how the current positioning supports the wellbeing of our colleagues
Cost	how the current positioning is keeping total costs low or high

Figure 22   Value impacts

At this point you can go as big or as small as you please. You might just want to take a small selection of value impacts (i.e., hone in on two or three that are important to you now). You might want to focus in on the value impact across a cohort, a specialist business unit, or a geography. Remember your systems architect mindset—break it down until you are comfortable with the scope and scale of the value drive review across the 3W equalisers you have selected. You may also want to add a value aspect that you don't feel is captured. That is okay. Go wild! You are the producer on the Mix Desk after all.

9

Time to Play

> 'It's a dangerous business, Frodo, going out your door. You step onto the road, and if you don't keep your feet, there's no knowing where you might be swept off to'.
>
> —*Bilbo, from* Lord of The Rings, *J. R. R. Tolkien*

Okay, we know where we are. We have our base 'mix'. We also know how that 'where' is impacting us positively, negatively or neutrally. Now it's time to play with where we could be, like to be or need to be into the future. I use these words purposefully. Often, where we would like to be can be at odds with where we need to be based on the impact that we need to create. At this point, however, it is all about the dream. The 'could be'. We need to take the guiderails off and think beyond the box—or at least think within a much bigger box!! Just like a producer playing around with some mixes that may or may not hit the spot, so too we are playing with experimental future work mixes that may open up meaningful paths to ideas and innovation. It is worth noting that Prince only had a basic 16-track mixing desk when he recorded one of his classic albums 'Dirty Mind', and the poor old Beatles only had a four-track recording of 'Revolver' (my personal Beatles album favourite), so with 16 equalisers to play with you should be at least able to produce something interesting!

Multiple Ways to Play

How to dream. Not easy. From our research at the Future of Work Institute (FOWI), most sessions end up focused 70% on challenges and criticisms, 20% on actions and often less than 10% on taking the time to dream or imagine. But you are in luck—thanks to the equalisers we have a structured model to work with that has imagination 'built in'. The right-hand side of each equaliser represents the 'extreme possible future' of that element. For example, dialling all the way up on the workforce 'blend' criteria means we will be harnessing all forms of employment types—from permanent to gig and fractional across all parts of the business in a very seamless and frictionless manner. From experience we would suggest utilising a few tried and tested approaches to break into the dreamer zone.

The Core (Classic): What If?

The 'what if?' question is the cornerstone of dreaming with the 3Ws and associated equalisers. Indeed, the 'what if?' question has become a go to for innovation practitioners for a very long time. Using this approach we focus on asking 'what if?' across the 3W equalisers. Taking one equaliser, we might say: 'What if our offices became more experiential?' Or it might be a little more pragmatic: 'What if we moved the "proposition" equaliser one step more to the right?' We can then discuss value impact the same way as we did for the current equaliser positions. To help, you can utilise some of the 'questions to ponder' connected to each of the metawaves that you saw earlier in the book.

Add Time, Space and Conditions

A useful way to go further and deeper with the 'what if?' question is to combine it with three dimensions (remembering our systems architect mindset). We can add in time, space and conditions to our exploration. Definitions for each are provided below, along with some examples.

- **Time**

  Definition: Refers to the temporal aspect of equaliser you are looking at. You might focus on putting a 5-year horizon on the 'what if?' if you really want to go strategic, or a much tighter timeframe of 12–18 months to get focused and action oriented. From experience, using multiple timelines can help—so you might look at a 5-year horizon but then hone in on years one and three in terms of where the dials may lie on the equalisers. But it's more than that. You might introduce other time aspects like seasonality. Think time across big time spans and small timeframes. Also ask: 'When does something need to be dialled to the left, when should it be dialled to the right?'

- **Space**

    Definition: Refers to the spatial aspect of the system (the where). You might focus on applying one of the equaliser shifts in a particular team, business unit, brand or geography. It may also be focused on a subset of an overall process or design. For example, you might want to hone in on one aspect of an evolved people value proposition, not on it all—perks and benefits, for example. You might hone in on one step of the career journey. Think about it as going up and going down. Different levels of resolution. You get the point!

- **Conditions**

    Definition: Refers to the different conditions that might drive a jump in the equaliser. For example, on the blend equaliser the focus might be seasonal. The business will utilise an existing contingent talent pool between November and December. It may look at using supplementary R&D contractors during new version updates, and so on. Focusing on different states and conditions can really drive different thinking and help you find new opportunities.

Dial Them All to the Right

To really move into the dream-like state, you might dial all the equalisers to the right (see Figure 23). This approach really helps to break through constraints and drive conversations around what all these changes could be for your organisation. You can then worry about why these dial-ups might not make sense after you have a conversation about why they do. Again, focusing the conversation on the impacts provided in Chapter 8 will help to keep you, if not grounded, then at least only partially floating!

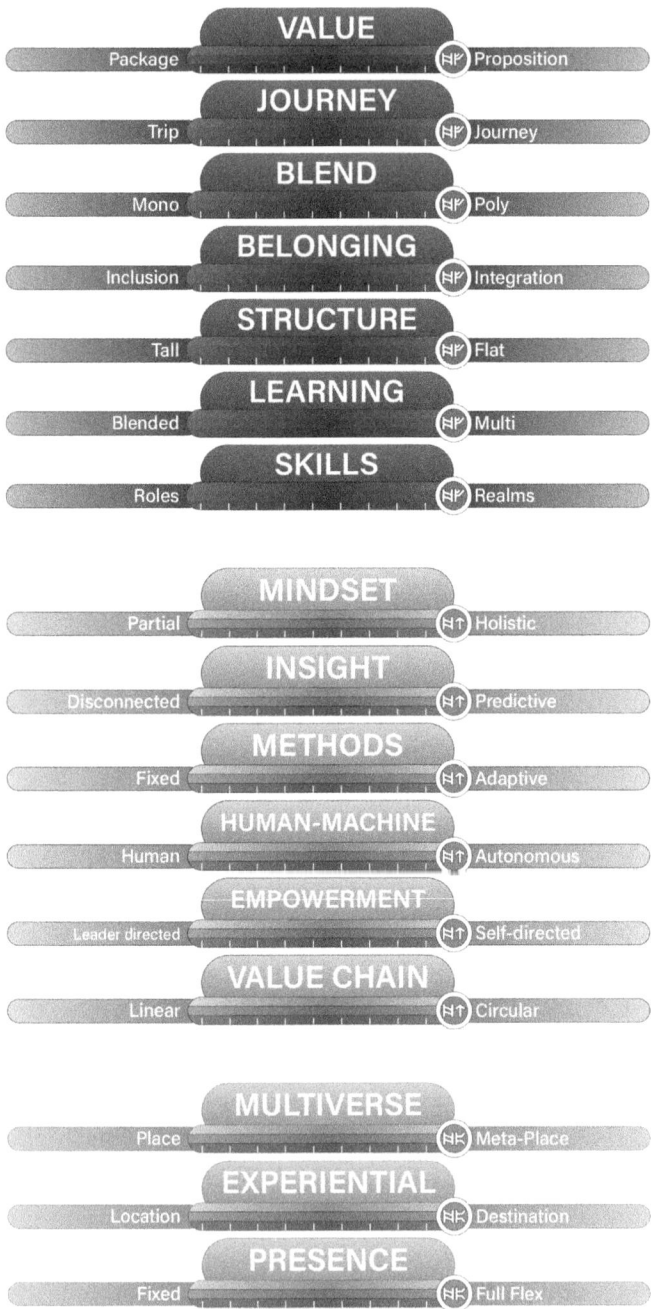

Figure 23 All dials to the right

Dial a Selection All the Way Up

If you don't want to go DEFCON 1, dial a few key equalisers up. Pick the equalisers that you feel you and your team have a lot of influence or control over. They might also be equalisers that you purposefully want to drive a bigger and more challenging conversation on (e.g., see Figure 24).

Solve a Big Challenge Forever

Another approach is to use the value impact drivers as a jumping-off point and hone in on a big challenge you want to 'solve forever'. The focus becomes about how far you might have to shift some or all the equalisers to solve a particular problem or challenge. The big problem might be around attraction. The challenge statement/solve a problem forever statement might be: 'How do we never have a Gen Z talent attraction problem again?' The focus can then turn to what equalisers would need to shift and by how much to solve the problem forever.

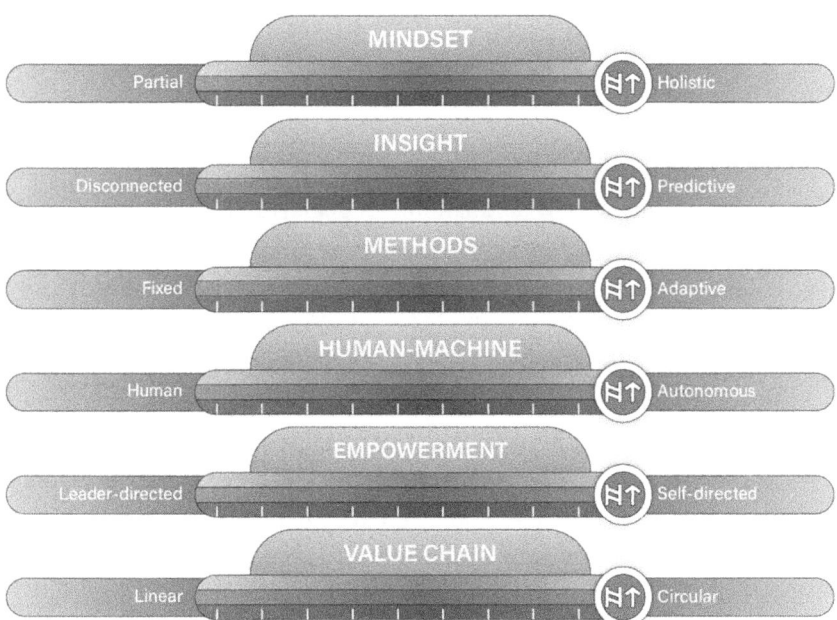

Figure 24   One W to the right

Go All or Nothing

Another, complementary, option is to utilise the concepts of ideals (derived from the TRIZ methodology and introduced to you as part of the systems architect mindset). Ask yourself, for each of the equalisers:

- What if we had all of it?
- What if we had none of it?
- What if it did it by itself?

Taking the human–machine equaliser as an example, we might ask:

- What if we had all key tasks automated?
- What if we had no people in that department?
- What if part of process X did everything by itself?

Combine this thinking with the time/space/conditions elements and you can really go broad on the dreaming side.

For the above approaches, make sure you follow some (ideally all) of the principles below:

- **Don't forget about the 'who'**

   Remember our destination designers mindset. We are always designing for a someone, or a group of someones (we could argue that we are now designing for a something in this meta human era, but let's not go there yet!). Think about the users as part of your explorations, as you might be thinking about a particular generation, or a specific neurodiverse group or a group connected with a particular competency or skill, even personality types. Either way, think about who the changes might affect. You will go deeper on this at the move stage but for the moment, just keep the users in your mind's eye.

- **Don't forget the colours either!**

   Don't forget the colours either! Remember your societal whisperer mindset. Have a look at the Appendix at the back of the book to help. Ask yourself: 'What would this shift in equaliser look like if it was more of a "green-code" approach than orange?' 'If our natural code in the organisation is more orange, how do we ensure the shift is in line with that code?' You can go as deep or as reflective as you like. Using the codes will take time as we all have a natural bias to a code, but it does help to change or evolve your thinking when you think through the codes.

- **Develop integral questions to get to new places**

     Integrating the above concepts, the following are useful follow-up question examples to follow the 'what if?'. Taking the 'What if our offices became more experiential?' (the destination equaliser) example, we might ask:

     - **(Space) Where would we dial it up?** *All our offices, or our spoke office, or one key office?*
     - **(Space) In what areas would we apply the dial-up?** *Might we make a part of one office more experiential to start?*
     - **(Destination designer) Who would we dial it up for?** *Who would we be making it more experiential for? What would more experiential mean for those groups of people?*
     - **(Impact) What would it impact positively and negatively**? *We might assume it improves retention and belonging. Possibly innovation. Will impact cost negatively if we overdo it?*
     - **(Time) When do we need to dial it up?** *Might we focus on destination concepts or designs at key times over the year and keep the office quite flexible during most of the year?*
     - **(Systems architect) What would be our first step?** *Get a team together to explore what more experiential might mean for one of our offices?*
     - **(Systems architect) How might it affect/interact with the other equalisers?** *Explore what other equalisers is interacts with—for example, the more experiential office might also then act as a third place for your contractor workforce.*
     - **(Societal whisper) If we looked at the design through primarily green and yellow codes, what might it mean?**

     These questions are only a sample set of jumping-off points to show how to bring in a fully integral approach. The key is to mix up the ideas above to get you to deeper and more interesting questions—otherwise, we end up in the same places that we have visited before.

And let's be honest, we don't want that. We are here to play first and worry later. Remember, the questions above only refer to one of our equalisers—you have 16 to play with. And multiple questions you can create and ask. You can go as deep, broad, narrow or shallow as makes sense for your context.

■ **Don't forget the value impact**

You have dreamed and created different mixes for your future work world but now it is time to come back down to earth, or at least come a little closer to earth. At this point you should know your base mx, have got to a place further than you might have thought possible as you have pushed the dials to their extremes, or taken a few selected ones and gone deep, solved a big problem or gone all 'ideal'. It's critical you link these imaginings back to the value impacts. Think about how changing each of the equalisers will impact one or more of the value factors. Map them, discuss them. You may also want to do a deeper dive and conduct some top-line research to understand how certain equalisers dialled to the left or right impacted other businesses. There is plenty of research out there on many of the equalisers, enabling you to go deeper to get a more precise view on potential impact.

■ **Use AI knowledge tools to inspire thinking**

Don't be afraid to use AI knowledge tools like ChatGPT to find and explore examples to support thinking. You can use the equalisers and associated definitions to find, by way of example, 'offices that fully utilise neuroarchitecture' or 'organisations using agile methods to improve HR onboarding' (bad prompts but you get the idea). Having examples in advance of a session can really help to bring the equalisers to life and help teams visualise what dialling up or down looks like. You can utilise the classic design—desirability, feasibility, viability—approach if you wish to put more structure on 'Why it makes sense to do this'. Use those three lenses to assess the equalisers you have a chance of making happen based on whatever value impacts or time horizons you have selected. Ask:

■ **Desirability:** Will people want this? (remember what people)
■ **Feasibility:** Can we do this? (is it possible in the time we have defined and the capabilities we have or need)

- **Viability:** Should we create this? (will it create the impact we require)

After this you should have a good idea of what mixes you want to bring forward. What equalisers you are convinced need to be dialled left or right to improve your mix and make your organisation more of a future work world. Now it's time to think about getting things to move. Or more precisely, getting people excited about your ideas and creating interventions to make things more real.

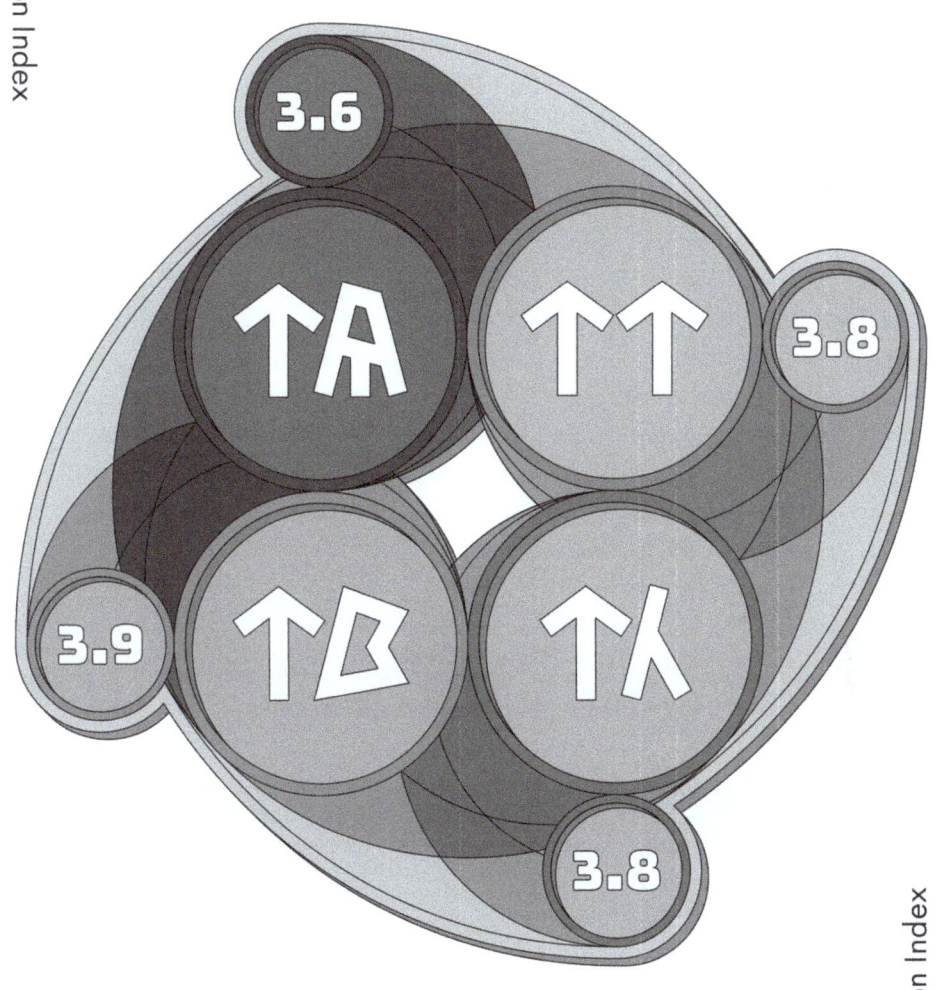

Jump 8: Transformation Index

End-of-year transformation huddle with business band member and orchestrator J. E. Pin.

Hi JE, how are you feeling?

To be honest, the whole thing feels a bit weird.

What do you mean?

Well, it's VERY different to my last place.

I know it can be hard to adjust to the transformation index and how we look at performance.

I'm a bit worried to be honest as I'm not even sure how I performed this year. I know I did some good stuff but the idea of the peer reflection with my team every month, the fact I'm a manager but not a manager if you know what I mean. The freedom and democracy is a bit of a double-edged sword. And the focus on transformation I get but equally it's very new to me.

Well, judging by the results I see here you seem to have had a very strong year. As you know, we look at four aspects of transformation for your yearly huddle: your own transformation (TOY); the transformation of your team (TOT); the transformation of the business (TOB); and the transformation of community (TOC). Here are your results:

	Score	Peer Av
Transformation of You	3.6	4
Transformation of Team	3.8	3.5
Transformation of Business	3.9	3.8
Transformation of Community	3.8	3.4

Surprised by that if I'm honest. I knew from speaking with the other band members they were happy with the level of support and new ideas I brought to the table over the year. Anvi told me how much the pieces of coaching helped her own performance—that is probably one of the things I'm most proud of this year.

To come back to your earlier point, I think the transformation focus is the hardest piece to get clear in people's heads when they join. So, by doing that coaching it is not coaching for coaching's sake but towards something bigger—about transforming that person's role in your band. That's why this organisation isn't for everyone. One thing to note is that your own transformation score is lower than that of your peers. From some of the analysis we can see you didn't tap into some of the wellness retreats and flexi work available. Your call of course. Hence the slightly lower TOY. The linguistic assessment did show an increase in Q4 of language normally associated with higher stress levels. Does that resonate with you?

Do you know, it makes some sense. I felt the last quarter I wasn't quite 'on it' as much as I normally am. I think this month I'm going to really use a few flex down days and one of the retreat credits. One thing I haven't really done is spent time on the upskill side. I'll have a look to see what makes sense.

I'd suggest you could link in with the skills performance coach and do a deep dive—it should help on that side of things. From a business transformation perspective, you nailed it—ahead of peers—and some of those spotlight projects really made a difference in terms of defects on the platform. It was one of the reasons your band shipped a lot of product this and last quarter. Well done.

Jin in the band is a real expert in self-management and agile ways of working so I asked him to lead up on those and really it is his win. His involvement made a big difference to getting some of those spotlight projects over the line.

Fantastic. You know how important community transformation is to us and your score in this area is incredible. It's a real testament to some of the impactful community initiatives you set up using the band community fund. One of the initiatives you worked on—updating that unused shop unit for micro businesses in collaboration with the local council—was a massive stand out. The council liaison called us to talk about the impact you made, and I know you spent a lot of your own time on the project.

This is one of the main reasons I actually joined this company. It was one of the few that is putting purpose into practice in a non-bullshit, apologies, non-gimmicky way. The community fund that each band can use is brilliant as we can agree on key projects that mean something to us all.

So overall a great year JE. You know that your bonus is made up of the impact across the four areas. This year TOC and TOB were prioritised by Dieter, so that will be reflected in your overall bonus along with team share bonus. You'll get that information later today and we can chat if needed, but it's very transparent and everyone will see the calculations. The business has been doing well so lots to shout about. Good luck with your goal setting this year.

This part of the book provides you with go-to strategies to get buy-in for your future work world mix and your dialled up/dialled down selection of equalisers. Chapter 10 focuses on harnessing next-level storytelling to drive meaningful emotional engagement and buy-in for change. Next-level storytelling refers to immersive storytelling approaches from areas like theatre, TV and theme parks. Some key concepts and ideas are introduced in how to use these powerful approaches in the real world. Chapter 11 focuses on creating 'spotlight' initiatives to test and learn some of the ideas generated by the mix phase. Told from practical experience, this chapter will give you the warts-and-all ways of getting something moving.

10 | Next-Level Storytelling

Now that we have our mix or mixes (if you're an overachiever) for our future work world, how do we inspire others to emotionally engage with them to drive change? How do we move from the classic death by over-telling (or to paraphrase Walt Disney, too much treatment and not enough treat) to a more experiential, exciting and enticing approach? The answer to our challenge is simple—next-level storytelling. The 'next-level' bit is not a gimmicky phrase but highlights the use of immersion and experiences to put the receiver into the story, or at least more into the story. To reference a quote by Jason Silva from the excellent book *Worlds of Wonder: Experience Design for Curious People* (Bar and Boshouwers, 2018): 'To make people feel something, you can't just communicate an idea. You've got to induce the feeling behind the idea'. And fortunately, we have a rich well to draw magic water from when it comes to creating immersive ways to engage internal (and external) audiences. Techniques that are seldom used within a business context. Techniques that come from places like TV, theme parks and theatre. And these approaches do not need to add cost—they are more about attention to detail and, most importantly, a commitment to rich storytelling. In the book *Disneyland Paris: From Sketch to Reality* (Littaye and Ghez, 2012), the authors highlight the importance Disney Imagineers (the people responsible for creating Disney theme parks) place on story:

> '. . . everything starts with a story at Walt Disney Imagineering. Every detail of every land in the park has to be backed up by a story, a "mythology"'

So now you know. Next-level storytelling is the key to change and that means moving away from classic presentational styles to more engaging story-based approaches. Here is how to do it (or at least some approaches to get you started), along with real-world strategies I have used in the Future of Work Institute (FOWI). As with all storytelling, these approaches can be as simple or as rich as you feel is required. Most, you will be glad to know, are low cost but all of them share one common objective—to craft a compelling story that is linked to an equaliser, or set of equalisers, that emotionally engages your audience to inspire meaningful change.

First Stop: The TV Show Bible

For those of you who don't know (and many don't), a TV show bible is a multi-page document that helps writers pitch their TV show. A properly put together one provides an in-depth blueprint of the show that includes the story world, tone, plots and an overview of key characters and so on, and how each develop from pilot to season one and beyond. It is, in many instances, highly visual and includes multiple images (see Figure 25) that really capture the look, feel and atmosphere of the show. In Hollywood-speak, the purpose of a show bible is to convince an executive or producer that the show is not just a one-off great piece of writing but has serious 'legs' (longevity). (A quick note here: show bibles are also a powerful tool to use in capturing the essence and culture of your organisation and can be a great basis for internal and external employee attraction and retention.)

A core foundation that anchors all good show bibles is the 'logline'. The logline is normally (with some variations) a one- or two-sentence summary of a TV show's total concept, intended to sum up its core conflict and the reason(s) why people would want to watch it. For example, here is the logline to *Stranger Things* that's doing the rounds on the internet. This may

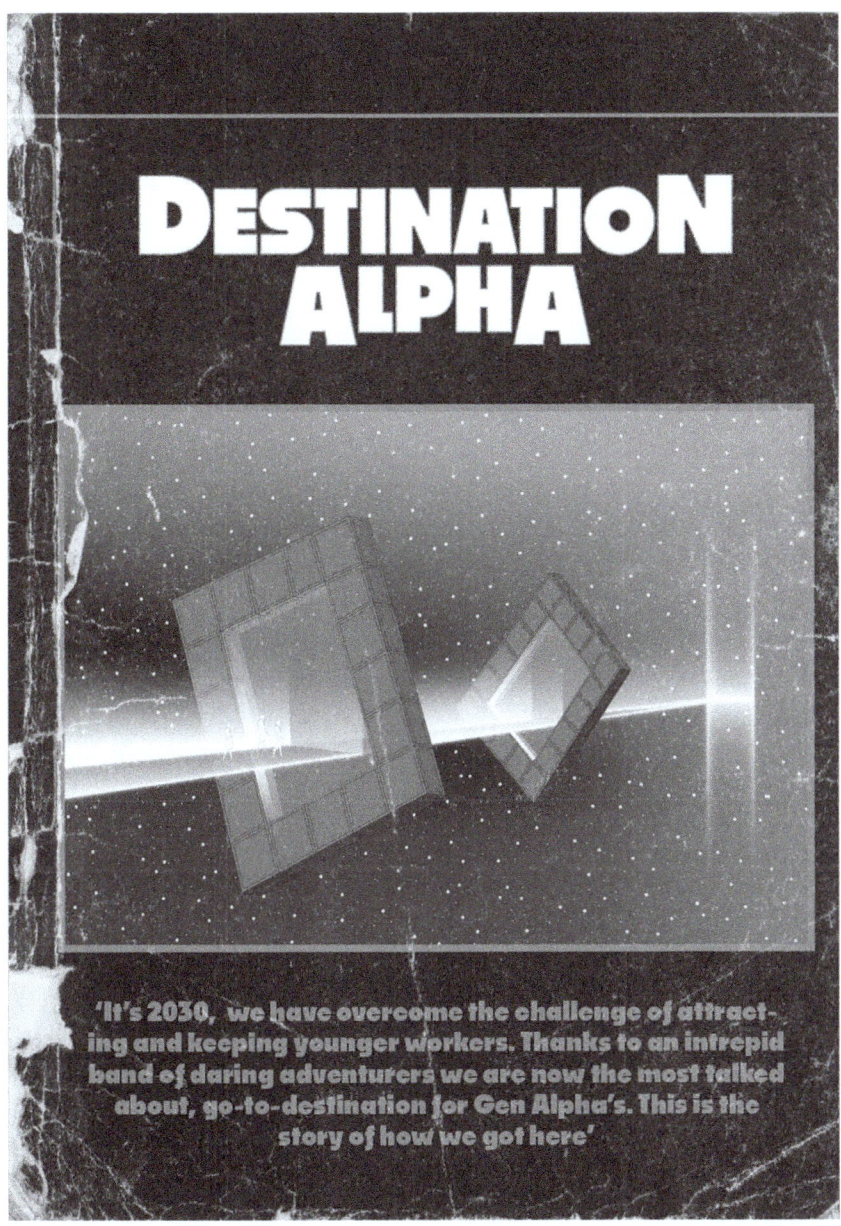

Figure 25 Fictional show bible cover

or may not be the official one, but it seems relatively accurate. (Yes, I am a *Stranger Things* fan, for reference):

> 'When a young boy disappears from a small town in the 1980s, his mother, a police chief, and his friends must confront terrifying supernatural forces in order to get him back'.

Notice a few things from the logline here: there is a location, a time setting (very useful), there is a call out of key characters and there is a form of conflict. Now, think about the logline idea in the context of your future work world. If there is a big-dial move on shifting your circular equaliser towards 'fully circular' (focused on the social side of ESG) to positively impact a key cohort (in this case children), you might create a logline like the following:

> 'With more than 30% of young children under the age of 5 globally not having enough food to eat daily in 2028, our leaders, our colleagues and our suppliers banded together to create one of the most ambitious and successful socially driven food programmes of our time'.

In this show bible you would think about some of the images you might use to highlight the challenge, but also to give a feeling of what the result would look like. You would highlight the key actors (in this case stakeholders) involved and the role they play within the story. You would also think about what Series 1 (in your case, stage one) might include.

Equally, the focus of the logline might be broader or, indeed, smaller. For example, you might have moved a lot of the equalisers to create a very different future work world mix to your current one. In that case, the logline will be based more on an overall story of change towards, perhaps, a logline based on a comprehensive future version of your organisation. Or it might be based on a key challenge you want to 'solve forever'. The example below highlights a potential logline focused on becoming a key destination for younger generations in the future:

> 'It's 2030, we have overcome the challenge of attracting and keeping younger workers. Thanks to an intrepid band of daring adventurers we are now the most talked about, go-to destination for Gen Alphas. This is the story of how we got here'.

The goal here is to create a logline that grabs attention, fully utilises a story approach and our destination designer's mindset. Note, in the example above, how it is noticeably clear who we are 'designing' our future work world for. The most important aspect, is that we have moved away from a mere presentational approach to a story-based approach to build upon. The logline engages at a much more emotional level.

The layout in Figure 26 can help you form a logline that will emotionally connect. It is based on and adapted from a Pixar storytelling structure with my additions. There are lots of different story structures, but I find this adapted one works in most situations. A word from the wise—your first few attempts will not be fantastic, but remember to link it to your future work world model and the key equalisers you have focused on shifting most significantly.

Remember, the logline is only part of the show bible. It will also include numerous visuals to get across the atmosphere of the story. Think about what visuals might represent the logline on which you have landed (see Figure 27). Are there AI-generated images you can quickly create to support that emotional connection? Have you existing in-house images you can modify to highlight that future? Also think about models here. For example, if one of the

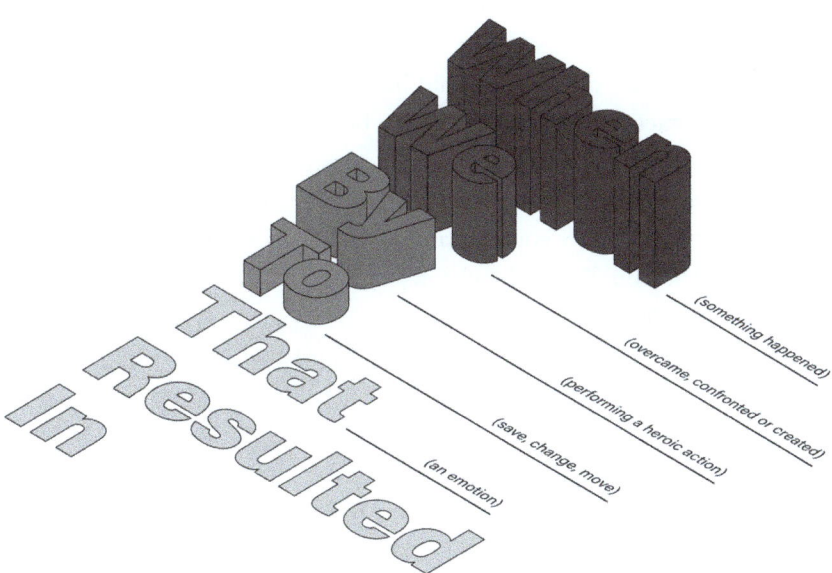

Figure 26 Adapted storytelling structure for your mix

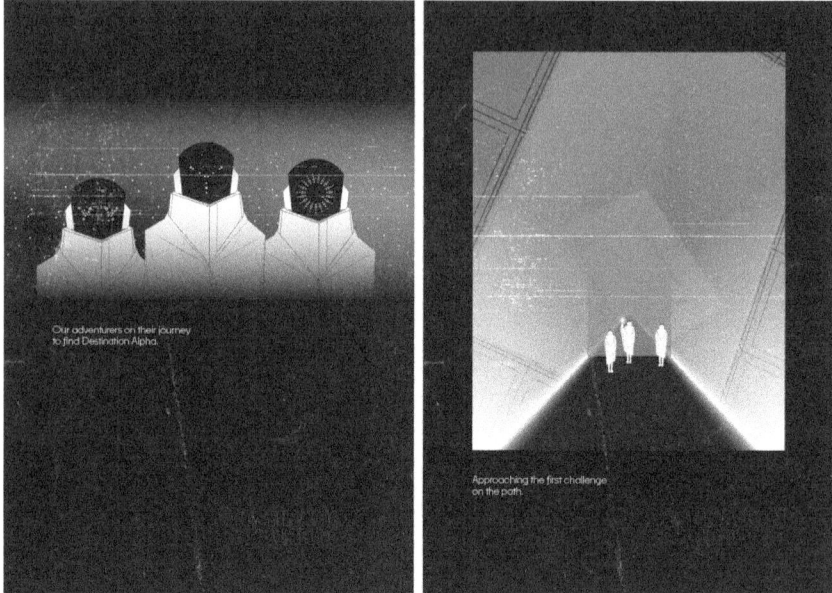

Figure 27　Visual focus of a show bible in Sci-Fi theme

equalisers you have ramped up is towards a more self-managed approach to
your teams as a key aspect of your future work world, find a model that shows
the principles behind being more self-managed. Think about what it would
feel like to self-manage. What would be difficult about it? You might create
a dummy character in your show bible who represents a 'self-manager'. The
idea of 'characters' is important. Characters can bring your future work
world to life. So don't be afraid to create one (or more). Your character
might be the audience you are trying to impact with your future work
world mix, they might also be characters/roles that don't currently exist in
your organisation.

　　To help build a character or a more personal level into your show
bible story it can be very useful to ask the following questions:

- What's in it/What will it mean for me? (individual level)
- What's in it/What will it mean for you? (other individuals/roles)
- What's in it/What will it mean for us? (team/unit level)
- What's in it/What will it mean for all? (organisational level)
- What's in it/What will it mean for them? (beyond organisational level)

This is a wonderful way to make the change in equalisers real at multiple levels. Even when doing this, remember to utilise the third-person view and use fictional characters. So, if you are going deep, for example, on what a shift in an equaliser will mean, to say a HR manager (other individuals/roles), you might hone in on one fictional character and talk through their story of change. For example:

> 'John is a grumpy sod, rarely upbeat, but loves one thing about his job. And that thing is Stir Fry Fridays. He also happens to be a HR manager with responsibility for D&I. And the changes have made his role "more bearable" to quote John himself'.

There are three key aspects about this character introduction to note. (1) John is fictional, he does not exist in the organisation. This is important, as you can technically use existing people in the organisation but this can be risky. Often, using a fictional character takes away any mental barriers to the core ideas you are attempting to get across. (2) It is a fun and authentic introduction, not the often used and linear '*This is John. He is a D&I HR manager*' approach. (3) It is unexpected and creates an immediate emotional and personal connection.

For all the talk that we are 'all storytellers at our core', taking a more story-driven approach can be hard if you aren't used to it. I've been told by various clients that it at once can be weird, embarrassing, fun, stupid, uncomfortable and exciting. But here is the thing. A story approach is a form of magic. Especially in an organisational context. People will forgive an average story if it's a story. They will often not forgive a decent old-school presentation because it is in their own comfort zone and is expected. Trust me (they say don't trust someone who says 'trust me', but there you go) when I say that a story-driven approach will drive more meaningful engagement, more emotional attachment and a higher probability of change. Because it is unexpected, a little messy and different. And the show bible is a good anchor approach to get you moving.

Humorous side note: One of my favourite humorous takes on a logline, in this case for a film, is one that was written for a TV magazine listing:

> 'Transported to a surreal landscape, a young girl kills the first person she meets then teams up with three strangers to kill again'.

If you haven't guessed it, it is *The Wizard of Oz*—funny but weirdly accurate! It eloquently shows the power of the logline and the multiple ways you can come at any story.

Second Stop: Themes

I love a good theme. Themes are like storytelling islands that make up your overall future work world. They connect the sometimes 'out there' logline to the more practical, the more get-able. When we talk about themes in this context we are not talking about things like death, remorse or happiness. We are talking about, normally, three to four core themes that will make the overall story real. Think of themes as the key containers that must be 'filled' and made real to get us to our end logline. That defeats our challenges. That enables our value impact. Think about Disneyland (yes, another theme park reference— but come on, it even calls out 'theme' in its description!). It has several themed lands that together make up Disneyland. And it's a similar concept here.

By way of example, suppose we have an organisation (based on a similar but generified FOWI project) with a future work world very much focused on the logline 'to be the most talked about, go-to destination for the Alpha Generation'. As part of our model phase, we might have looked at ramping up several key equalisers. We might have gone deep on the 'proposition' equaliser and turned it to the right, especially in relation to culture and engagement. We may also have looked at increasing the blend that we use to tap into early graduate students who want to work in a more part-time or flexible way, and we may have gone deep on the 'belonging' and 'value chain' equalisers, with a deep focus on meaningful social integration with the business. In a way, these have become the key enablers supporting achievement of the logline. But we want to turn these broad concepts into more story-driven themes that can engage and excite. So, we focus on developing our three core themes, as per Figure 28:

- **Playful Place:** Focus to create a more engaging, fun and informal approach to work.
- **Many Paths:** Blending new journeys that give graduates an opportunity to work part-time initially, then move into a contract model, then potentially into a full-time role or an active talent pool.

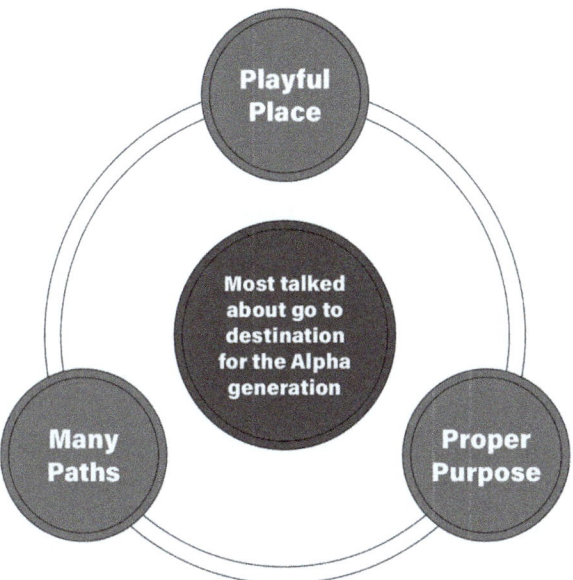

Figure 28 Three themes example

- **Proper Purpose:** Focus on ensuring better links between core goals and the development of the more meaningful social impact programmes that are important to Gen Alphas.

As the themes themselves are story led, they create more of an emotional connection along with the logline idea. They are also more strategic in that they are not 'an initiative' but a core theme that directs focus and energy over a long-term horizon. Multiple, diverse and innovative spotlight projects (you will read more on these later) can be designed, trialled and delivered to make the theme more real.

Third Stop: Artefacts

Picture the scene. A leadership group is expecting a standard deep-dive working session on the future of inclusion in their organisation. They are thinking about what it might mean to ramp it up into the future (based on the belonging equaliser in their future work world mix). A variety of views abound on the idea. Some think they are doing too much, some too little, some think they are doing enough. Others aren't sure about the business benefits, the link to their future and if the whole thing needs a re-think or a revolution. Classic Goldilocks zone. They are expecting some presentations, Post-its, standing around flip charts—you know the drill. As they enter the room, they are surprised, instead, to find a flag on a pole in the middle of the space. A flag they haven't seen before. One of the execs thinks they may have stumbled into the wrong room—perhaps received the wrong room number for the session. But no, they are in the right place. An introduction kicks in on a screen highlighting how this flag is their flag, and it represents that their organisation is at the leading edge of inclusive and integral practices. 'What does integral mean', murmurs one of the execs. They learn about a new 'integral inclusive' standard that doesn't exist yet. They learn that this new standard has created multiple advantages for their business. A selected few pages of the standard lie on the table. There is also a deep description of the flag, who designed it, what it means. The group is intrigued, energised and a little excited. They are ready to listen, to learn, to imagine and to act.

This example highlights the formidable power of the artefact. An artefact is an object, linked to the movement of one or more of our model equalisers, that represents in one 'thing' an image of a possible future realised. Need to get across the pressing need to take sustainability seriously in your business? Fill an office with a simulation of a day's waste of toilet paper (see Figure 29).

Need to really drive home the power of having a fully designed value proposition? Make up a competitor company and bring your team through their idealised EVP and it will get them moving. An artefact, can be many things. Here's a list of the different types of artefacts that will give you some jumping-off inspirations:

- **A physical object**—like a flag or another object that people can touch and feel.
- **A digital or virtual item**—an interactive platform, or avatar, or an alternate future website.
- **A story**—a story that gets across an equaliser shift but told through a narrative, a magazine article, an interview, even an ad.
- **Sound(s)**—often forgotten about, sounds, music, even pre-recorded voices can be very powerful to create an emotion.

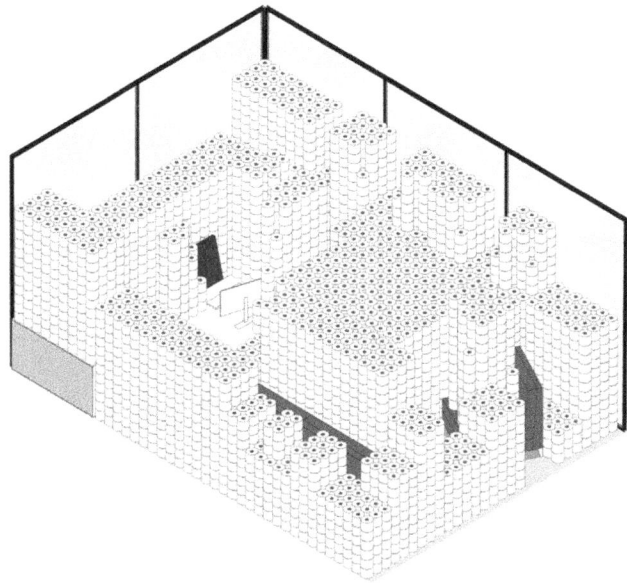

Figure 29   Toilet rolls galore!

- **An experience/encounter**—an unexpected encounter or experience, maybe a live interview, a challenge or a specific experience based on one of the equaliser shifts.
- **People**—who might represent a future role or their experience of working in your future work world.
- **A model**—often under-utilised, leading-edge models shine a new light or a new language (e.g., a 'self-management model' that introduces new principles of working to an agile team).
- **An 'alternative'**—creating a competitor that might be your main talent challenger, or an alternative company based on your future shifts.

At FOWI we utilise artefacts all the time. We have created interviews with a fictional future CEO and created businesses that don't exist. We have designed rooms that immerse leaders in a particular aspect of their future work world. We have created magazines from the future with a spotlight story on our client companies. We have created AI characters that represent how the work will be delivered in the near future. Creating an artefact is not necessarily expensive. But they can take a little time to land on something that connects what you are trying to achieve with your future work world mix. They are a powerful tool to create meaningful discussion and change.

Start by reflecting on the nine trips to the near fictional future that are randomly scattered throughout the book (Jumps 1–9). Use them as a jumping-off (no pun intended!) point for some ideas. For example, if you want to really dial up your use of the blend in your company to increase access to knowledge workers, play around with Jump 5. Link the story to your future work world. How might it work in your context? How can you bring it to life within your R&D group, by way of example. It might be a written interview in a magazine with a fictional expert in a knowledge domain that is important to you and how he/she/them is working within the new blended model structure in your business. You can go further and use an actor if needed. You could also make up a competitor company (fictional or otherwise) that is really harnessing the blend and 'kicking your butts' when it comes to innovation impact.

Note that whilst the primary focus of the artefacts (jumps) in this book is firmly on a near fictional future, they are a powerful tool to get across the past and present of an organisation. You can use artefacts to emphasise a key point on a current challenge or situation equally. Or use an artefact to escalate an impending change, or an external metawave.

Feel free to utilise all and more of the approaches highlighted. The most important thing is to turn your future work world mix into more than a mix. Transform it into an emotionally engaging story but with a serious business side. You simply cannot be a 'destination designer' without understanding the power of next-level storytelling. And this chapter is only the tip of the iceberg. I implore you to dive into the depths of the oceans of story techniques available to you. You'll be surprised at what you will find.

11 | Spotlight Initiatives

Spotlight initiatives are all about designing, learning and experimenting. Playing around with how the equalisers you have ramped up or down might look in the real world. Wearing our destination designer mindset, we might call this prototyping, or user testing. There is a huge knowledge base available on this stuff—from business experimentation to service design to agile methodologies. For my money, Stefan H. Thomke's *Experimentation Works* is still the grandaddy of them all when it comes to the ultimate guide to business testing—seek it out NOW. For our purposes, I'm going to focus on what has worked for myself and the team at the Future of Work Institute (FOWI) and simplify the approach as much as possible for real-world use.

Fundamentally, spotlight initiatives help us to better understand how a concept might look and work in the real world. In fact, 'How might it work in the real world?' is probably the most useful guiding question when it comes to spotlight initiatives. But they are, and should be, more than that. They are a powerful way to create sustainable buy-in for much larger-scale change. A spotlight initiative can be:

- **Going deeper** on an equaliser and developing an operating framework, processes or model to see how things might look within the realities of your organisation.

- **Co-creating** with the user or employee group you have focused on with the initiative to come up with evolved designs.
- **Developing** a small, tight project in a specific area to evaluate a specific hypothesis or idea.
- **Re-designing/Re-energising** an existing initiative in line with some of the learnings from the mindset, metawave or model stage.

Thinking about ramping up automation to increase productivity (the human–machine equaliser)? Then try one form of AI-based automation, in one area of business, for one type of user. Thinking of improving your PVP for the younger generations in your business? Then get one group of young gens together and play it out. Thinking of introducing self-management, then pick one team in one area and start with three or four core principles of self-management. Uncomfortable about the lack of detail for a new service concept around learning and development? Then do a much deeper dive to explore the mechanics of how it might work. Want to explore a more holistic method of performance management (the mindset equaliser), then take your existing performance indicators, tear them apart, re-build and trial. The goal here is to learn and from that move forward into a deeper form of design or implementation.

At the FOWI we have created four guiding principles to help in the selection of the deeper-dive spotlight projects. Use these as the next step, after your mix-phase prioritisation.

1. **It makes one of our key equaliser changes more real**

    Ultimately, conducting a spotlight initiative is about moving one of the equalisers forward that we have identified in the mix phase of our future work world. Moving an equaliser forward might mean getting to a deeper understanding of how it might work in practice, implementing a small aspect of the overall continuum to learn, like in the examples given above. It might take a few spotlight initiatives to make the changes. What's important here is to understand that 'making it real' can mean that what you started with might be very different by the time it gets to a level of realisation. It's important to be okay with that. Take the win of modified real-world realisation instead of losing momentum due to biased theoretical inflexibility.

2. **In a small way it defeats a big challenge or drives value impact**

The spotlight initiative needs to be focused at least in a small way on defeating a major challenge in the business that you identified in the mix stage. Remember the 'defeat a challenge forever' approach and the value impacts you have identified by moving the equalisers. If, for example, attracting more mature workers is a major challenge, and we have looked at new part-time working models as part of our blend equaliser, then the spotlight project needs to focus on how that model will (even in a small way) go towards solving that problem whilst driving improvement in the value impact drivers you have defined. In this case, the small project might be focused on impact over a 3-month period in one area of the business. This will provide enough initial evidence to push on with possibly a larger-scale project. The key here is to keep the measures of success simple and small. One or two key measures are all you need at this point.

3. **Will have high 'EQ' impact beyond HQ or unit or site**

This is a key principle that is often missed in other approaches to testing and experimenting. The initial spotlight initiatives should not only have wide-reaching application but also have a high emotional aspect. In other words, it needs to tap into the zeitgeist of the business on stuff that really matters at an emotional level. If your business is really struggling to attract skilled workers in a particular business area, this has a real emotional impact on the team leaders trying to deliver results for your business. There is already a high emotional connection to the solution of that challenge. A small win in a high 'EQ' area will enable real momentum and an appetite for further work in the area.

4. **Can be fairly boundaryless (in team and thought)**

This one might feel obvious but is often missed. It is important that spotlight projects can cover the span of teams that the spotlight project affects—not necessarily just the users you have focused on. Taking the skilled workers example, you need to be able to include resourcing managers, recruiters, existing skilled workers, marketing and more. It is also important that the spotlight initiative you have selected can tap into knowledge and ideas beyond the obvious and allow these ideas as part of the scoping project. Remember, at the model stage we have imagined a lot, so we need to maintain a level of creativity throughout the process.

Creating the Spotlight Initiative: Cheat Sheet

A good spotlight initiative should have a simple one or two pages associated with it. It does not need lots of information but the right information. You will have already discussed a lot of this as part of your 'mix phase' but this is where you go deeper and get to a more practical, actionable place. Highlighted below are some of the areas that should be included, along with useful descriptions and pointers to guide you on your way.

1. **Type of spotlight initiative**

   Is the spotlight a deeper dive on one of the equalisers to find out more, is it a small, applied testing project, is it a more fully formed model that can be further critiqued? Be clear on what it is. Look for the lowest common denominator that moves you closer to getting to the equaliser setting.

2. **User focus**

   Who is the spotlight project going to impact? Who is it for? If there are more 'users', make sure they are considered as part of the initiative. Or create another linked spotlight initiative with a different user group if that makes sense. Also, highlight how you are going to involve the users as part of the spotlight initiative

3. **Value impacts and challenge to solve**

   What challenge does this spotlight initiative go towards solving? What key value drivers will it impact initially and eventually. You will have the value impact elements from the mix phase, but you might need to go a bit deeper here and perhaps conduct some desk-based AI information gathering to understand the likely scale of impacts. For example, having a clearly defined employee value proposition could increase your level of retention by 10–20% based on a quick scan of research, and attraction by 20–30%. Get at least a sense of the level of impact at this stage.

4. **Hypothesis to test or questions to answer**

   Be clear on sub-hypotheses and questions you want to prove or answer as part of the spotlight initiative. You may, for example, have a hypothesis that a 'new benefit designed for the 18–25 cohort will increase benefit use by at least 20% as a subset initiative under the "proposition" equaliser'. You may have a few key questions related to that equaliser and that cohort you may want to answer. You don't necessarily need to have a hypothesis or questions if you have very clear value impacts and challenges defined, but it can be useful if you want to go a little deeper on things.

5. **Prototype approach**

   Here, think about the type of prototyping you are going to utilise. There are loads of options available. If it is an early-stage deeper dive on a particular equaliser, then it is more likely that using tools like storyboards, process flows and models will be more than enough to get to a deeper level of understanding. If you are going a little further and you want to actually develop a small project, then it is important to define that project in more detail. For example, if you are exploring an 'expertise by the hour' model for your innovation teams, this becomes more of an official project where you might start with five to ten outside experts willing to take part in the project and you focus their expertise on an initial maximum number of hours (say 20 hours) on one particular project that might be at early stages. In this case, you still need to be clear about the value impacts and must involve both the providers (the experts by the hour) and the users (the innovation team). Be clear on the approach you are going to take. The more into execution you go, the more spotlight initiative management and time you will need to ensure success.

6. **Testing and measures**

   Think here about how long the spotlight initiative is for. If it's more of a deep dive on design, then that might only be 3–4 weeks, or even a day. If it's more of a project-based spotlight initiative, like the R&D example, then you might need 3 months or more. As part of this you also need to think about how you will capture success or learnings. Are you going to use a questionnaire, interviews? Can you capture key moments that highlight the success of the spotlight initiative. Can you link it obviously back to a key data point. What is useful here is to find a mix of qualitative and quantitative data. If, for example, you are working on a spotlight initiative focused on attracting more mature workers, then one of our core quantitative measures would be the number of new CVs submitted from more mature candidates. You may also supplement this with a survey to understand how those candidates felt throughout the front-end recruitment process and how it engaged and excited them about the prospects of working with the hiring organisation. This rounded approach gives you a full view of the success of the spotlight initiative.

A Word on the Power Models: Any Model

The more astute reader will probably have guessed at this point that I have a huge admiration for Walt Disney, especially his work that led to the creation of the first true theme park. He has something perhaps unexpected in common with another colossus I admire and a major figure in musical theatre—Andrew Lloyd Weber. Creator, with Tim Rice, of my favourite concept album of all time, and subsequent musical juggernaut—'Jesus Christ Superstar'. Miniatures and models played a significant role in both of their creative journeys. Weber, at the age of 7 or 8 (according to his excellent biography), created a toy theatre where he would stage miniature productions. Even going so far as to use a revolving stage! Disney, inspired by a trip to the Thorne exhibit at the Golden Gate International Exposition in San Francisco in 1939, got into miniatures in a big way. He built a small-scale railway in his backyard, the Carolwood Pacific, crafted pint-sized potbellied stoves and even exhibited a miniature cabin at the Festival of California Living at the Pan Pacific Auditorium in Los Angeles in 1952. He went on to fully utilise models of all types in designing Disneyland.

Models are a seriously powerful tool in helping to visualise, critique and imagine. Whatever spotlight initiative you are exploring, don't be afraid to create a model. Any model. It might be a storyboard to understand a new employee journey you are creating; it might be a paper-based model to play around with a new employee interface. It might even be a model that helps you play around with a new team meeting or facilitation. Be like Disney and Weber. Use the power of models to create and learn.

Do or Do Not. There Is No Try

Yoda, Jedi Master, rarely gets it wrong with his quotes. And I can't think of a better quote to end this chapter (and indeed the book—yes, there is a conclusion after this, but it's brief). Ultimately, 'move' is about getting things going, taking action. It might be that the action is a compelling story to get your team to think differently about one equaliser. Or an absolute epic to kick the organisation into the future. It might be a step into a new knowledge source to look at things from a different angle. A rough model or concept. Perhaps a working concept to test things out over a day, a week or months! They are all relevant. They will take you in the direction of a future work world that will excite, entice and engage. Do or do not? There is only do.

Jump 9: 'Reframement' (The New Retirement)

A new word for a new era—opinion piece extract on aging workers in the European Union (2029).

It's only 5 years since Katherine Coburn coined the phrase 'reframement' as an alternative to 'retirement', but it's caught on. And this shouldn't be surprising. With the European Union's old-age dependency ratio hitting 40% (in other words, they will have only a little more than two persons of working age for every person aged 67 years or more), employers are changing their views on older, more mature workers. And older workers are changing their views too. In her recent book *From Good to Grey-T*—a humorous play on Jim Collin's classic title—Coburn highlights how less than 26% of older workers now want to fully retire at the age of 67, and are keen for employers to create or 'reframe' (hence the term) how they enable older workers to continue in employment.

Jan, now 71, is a fractional leader at a small independent prop manufacturer, based in the Netherlands, for the theme park industry. Unlike the 'can't teach an old dog new tricks' stereotypes often ascribed to more mature workers, he has continuously re-skilled and is a major contributor to the business. CEO Roly Timp calls him 'our wisdom warrior' and states that '15 hours of Jan's time a week is worth more than 40 hours of most everyone else's'. Jan also fits in some coaching with another small firm—but this is, according to Jan, more 'intermittent and based on specific need'. Jan is one of a growing number of 'reframers' literally wearing their new status on their sleeves. Last year, famed jewellery designer (and reframer) L. M. Win created a pin and cufflink set representing this new 'wisdom tribe' and they have become quite the status symbol with more mature workers.

And employers need people like Jan. With a growing 'aging but healthy' over-65 population and an overall decrease in births, employers have no choice but to change the workforce playing field. One such organisation,

Experientual, has implemented what it calls the 'second-curve' programme. This programme enables over-67s to choose a new reframed career path within the business, capped at 23 hours per week, but in a new area. Due to tax breaks and the new pension scheme, these workers can still draw down a percentage of their pension whilst being paid by their employer, with limited tax implications.

Leader of the programme Johan Strunman likes to think of it as a 'new type of apprenticeship'. Some become coaches within the business, others upskill in a totally new area, others will undertake special projects. Even when this second curve comes to an end, it's not the end of the story. Far from it. Experientual has established Reframement Resource Groups for people who have moved beyond the business. These resource groups, a little like a mix between 'People's Sheds' and modern social clubs, create an ongoing connection that still enables ex-employees to work on social and special projects in a volunteer capacity. These programmes have been in place now for the past 3 years and the success has meant continued investment and an expansion of the programme into other parts of the business.

According to Katherine Coburn: 'The future is grey—and not in a bad way. If we can find more innovative ways to make work enticing, exciting and engaging for more mature workers, we can genuinely drive greater competitive advantages for the organisations we work with'.

Conclusion

If you have made it this far, I hope it is because you enjoyed the trip. Or you might just be very conscientious, always completing reading journeys regardless of the relative blandness of travel. For whatever reason, we find ourselves here, together, at the end. The last of my first.

Conclusions are difficult to write. In a way, they are more than simple closure. They represent a form of hope. A hope that the preceding pages will resonate with diverse and curious minds amongst the ever-surging digital ocean of novel ideas. The greatest conclusion to a book—in this case, a novel— comes from *Post Office* (1971) by Charles Bukowski: 'In the morning it was morning, and I was still alive. Maybe I'll write a novel, I thought. And then I did'. Beautiful. Simple. The stripped back literary magic of Bukowski eludes me. Nor is this one of the great novels. But I can at least try to keep this conclusion simple.

Think. Mix. Do.

In a way, these three words are the conclusion. We are, all of us, writing the future of work story, and every leader can be a contributor to the next great chapter for their organisations. Think in the most holistic way possible—be a systems architect, destination designer and societal whisperer all at once. Mix and re-mix your future work world and be fearless in imagining all sorts of possibilities that will engage, entice and excite. And do! Create stories that drive action. Do that weird pilot. Go deep on those nuggets of knowledge from unexpected places. Change and re-think that initiative that doesn't feel quite right

It is impossible to be an expert across the future of work. At least as it's defined in the book. And I include myself in this. This gives me great solace. And it should give you great solace too. To re-quote the great Shunryu Suzukiln: 'In the beginner's mind there are many possibilities, but in the expert's mind there are few'. Depending on your own expertise in key areas, you might find some of my observations and perspectives amateurish, some innovative and insightful, others routinely professional. I am okay with this. The focus has been to create an engaging user and design guide across the broadest future of work vista possible. Harnessing my eclectic mix of expertise and experiences. To stretch thinking. To stimulate mixing. And in that, at least, I hope I've succeeded.

Thank you for taking this trip with me. Over to you. Over and out.

Notes

Foreword

1. At the time of writing, AI-produced, arranged, composed and performed albums are a thing. Velvet Sundown, an AI-generated band, had amassed over one million streams on Spotify as of 2025.

Structure

1. Paul Brady. Song: The World Is What You Make It. First released in 1995. Available on the 1999 compilation album, Nobody Knows: The Best of Paul Brady. Rykodisc.

Part 1: Mindset

1. Disclaimer: Sounding intelligent on the future of work is no guarantee of popularity at parties. In fact, it may have the opposite effect!

Chapter 1: Mindset One: The Systems Architect

1. This definition comes from the author's work initially developed in 2021 and further evolved via his supplementary work at the Future of Work Institute (FOWI).
2. A project led by the author resulting in a whitepaper. https://landing.cpl.com/future-of-work/future-of-work-world.html
3. Note: The jumps highlighted in this example are based on Pine's (1999, updated 2024) concept of the move from products to services, to experiences to transformations.

4. Altshuller actually refers to the 'IFR' or 'Ideal Final Result' in this quote but for simplicity's sake Ideality is a good proxy.

Chapter 2: Mindset Two: The Societal Whisperer

1. Note: In this section you will see references to 'turquoise' code and 'teal'. The term teal comes from Frederic Laloux's work on organisational evolution, inspired partly by spiral dynamics but not identical. Think of teal as a blend of yellow and turquoise codes applied in an organisational context. I refer to teal when speaking in terms of business DNA throughout the latter parts of this chapter.
2. Author's note: I would advise the reader to refer fully to the Appendix as a key part of reading this chapter.
3. Fortune CHRO, 17th February 2023. Amber Burton & Paolo Confino.

Chapter 3: Mindset Three: The Destination Designer

1. A broader play on the phrase 'nothing about us without us', a phrase that likely emerged from Eastern Europe and was later popularised by James Charlton in the 1990s as part of the disability rights movement.

Chapter 5: Workplace

1. https://www.brickfanatics.com/lego-starts-world-largest-library-bricks/

Chapter 6: Worktask

1. 'Now when you pick a pawpaw, Or a prickly pear, And you prick a raw paw, Well, next time beware, Don't pick the prickly pear by the paw, When you pick a pear, Try to use the claw, But you don't need to use the claw, When you pick a pair of the big pawpaw', Bare Necessities (*Jungle Book*, 1967).
2. When Civil War II (2016) left Iron Man in a deep coma, that AI activated in 'Infamous Iron Man' (2016) #1 by Brian Michael Bendis and Alex Maleev.

Appendix

1. Descriptions and overviews derived and adapted from spiral dynamics references in the Bibliography, combined with author's own contributions and additions from practical use.

Appendices

Value Systems[1]

This appendix gives a deeper dive of the value systems from the societal whisperer mindset. For the orange, green, yellow and turquoise codes, talent journey examples are provided to highlight practical use. Remember, as per your mindset, that your designs for now and next will likely be a 'technicolour mix'!

Value systems change as we evolve individually and as societies, which is reflected in changing behaviours, goals, motivations, expectations and so on.

In evolving order, the value systems are described as follows:

- Beige—survival, pure focus on physical needs.
- Purple—tribal, basic sense of community emerges.
- Red—dominative, strong sense of polarisation between rulers and those ruled.
- Blue—absolutistic, systematic order is kept through compliance and hierarchy.
- Orange—achievistic, success is strived towards; skills, competition and optimisation.
- Green—sociocentric, a collaborative spirit for the common good.
- Yellow—empowered; innovationand imagination are expressions of self-development.
- Turquoise—interconnected, synergistic, where everything is a co-dependent system, utilising the best of all codes.

Each value system has a predominant skillset, mindset, structure and communication.

Beige
Survival

This value system, characterised by limited self-awareness, relies on instincts and habits to survive. Motivated by food, water, warmth, sex and safety.

All energy is directed towards survival through innate sensory abilities and instinctual reactions. In principle, in beige there are no typical leadership characteristics.

An individual is only directed towards the self. Teamwork doesn't exist, except for the moment of transition into the purple tribalistic value system, when some type of teamwork is emerging in order to survive.

Characteristics
- Driven by biological, physiological and instinctual needs.
- Strong reflexes, motor skills and highly developed physical senses.
- All value systems may experience beige as dependent, inadvisable and needy, but also as a form of unreasonableness in its drive for survival.

Core Values
Being attentive to various methods and scenarios of surviving and taking care of oneself.

Negative Associations
Very limited scope, focus solely on oneself in terms of survival.

Examples
Newborn baby, chronic patients, farmers in feudal times.

This is a group-oriented system, in which people sacrifice individual needs for the tribe, the elders and the ancient ways. Motivated by strong allegiance to chief, elders, ancestors and individual subsumed into the group.

There is strong emphasis put on respect of all that is and was and attention to the emotional (personal and/or family) bonds between people. Reverence of objects, places, events, rites and customs as part of keeping the group's integrity.

Characteristics
- Unconditional acceptance and loyalty by members.
- Emotional connection (a sense of family).
- A very strong group identity.
- The group serves as a protection from the outside world.

Core Values
Peace, natural, safe, emotional, trust.

Negative Associations
Closed, evasive, fearful, conservative. Stick together in close groups. Keep everything within the boundaries of the community. Avoid confrontations.

Examples
Tribes, sports teams, hobby/enthusiast groups (sport supporters), religious groups in the initial stage.

Red
Dominative

For red, 'life is a battleground' with winners and losers. The red value system is driven by achieving goals and reaching objectives through decisive moves that don't consider minorities or other parties other than the alliance. Strong focus on victory and power (over the whole process and participants) using domination, exploitation and conquest as its methods.

It is focused on the end goal only, therefore utterly lacking empathy, guilt or remorse. Keen to beat, conquer, out-fox and dominate others.

Characteristics
- Following impulses.
- Displaying power.
- 'I orientation', dominance, power and oppression.
- Strives for self-preservation and fear.
- Free from guilt or shame.
- Loyal to those who are considered friends.

- Decisive and energetic.
- Enforcement by way of sanctions.
- 'If you are not with us, you are against us'.

Core Values
Decisive, effective, conquering, victorious, unscrupulous.

Negative Associations
Forceful, inconsiderate, ruthless, creating inequalities, lacks empathy.

Examples
Dictators, army on the battlefield, narcissistic business leaders.

Blue
Absolutistic

The blue value system can be described as very traditional and bureaucratic. Built around established societal norms, process, absolute order and authority figures. The key behaviour is compliance, adherence to rules constitutions, commandments, laws or codes and obedience towards the higher principle.

Safety, uniformity and predictability are considered a great value and serve as a guideline for progress, which allows mostly incremental steps. Laws, regulations and discipline build character and moral fibre. Children should be educated to follow rules, to conform and conserve the system.

Characteristics
- Discipline, duty, self-control.
- Order, routine, security.
- Compliance with the doctrine and the rules.
- Absolute, literal, definite.
- Hierarchy, structures of authorities, bureaucracy.

Core Values
Secure, accountable, predictable, uniform, structured.

Negative Associations
Bureaucratic, emotionally detached, lacks diversity, risk averse, need to trust, same experience everywhere, inducing guilt.

Examples
Government and administrative institutions, church.

Optimisation and a strong belief in science and rationality define this highly achievement-oriented value system, especially towards materialistic gains. The laws of science rule politics, the economy and human events. The main drive behind people's action is a desire to win better positions in comparison to potential rivals.

Societies prosper through strategy, technology and competitiveness. Earth's resources should be used to create and spread the abundant good life. For that reason, obtaining higher status (both financial and social) and good self-image become the basic motivation. Some of the main tools to achieve this would include active competition, risk taking and excellence.

Characteristics
- Rational and pragmatic.
- Competitive.
- Elitist, image-sensitive (status and recognition).
- Ambitious and striving for excellence and success.
- Materialistic.
- Focused on results, growth and efficiency.

Core Values
Results driven, pragmatic, risk oriented, premium, explorative, agile, efficient, optimisation.

Negative Associations
Self-reliant and uncollaborative, calculative, focused only on tangibles, opportunistic, manipulative, quotas oriented.

The Talent Journey through the Orange Lens Integrating Ideality and Contradiction Tensions

- **Attraction**

  Ideality: Fast, low to zero cost, high-quality sourcing with no bias.
  Contradiction: Speed versus fairness
  Resolution Examples: Use ML for efficiency but add bias-audit layer; separate AI speed from human fairness checks.

- **Onboarding**

  Ideality: Instant productivity, zero downtime.
  Contradiction: Depth versus speed (comprehensive training slows productivity).
  Resolution Examples: Parallelise—use micro-learning embedded in daily work, so learning and productivity happen together.

- **Retention**

  Ideality: Reward-linked performance drives loyalty.
  Contradiction: Recognition speed versus cultural authenticity (incentives can feel transactional).
  Resolution Examples: Introduce transparent performance dashboards + peer recognition (monetary + social).

- **Leaving**

  Ideality: Zero disruption; all alumni pipeline remains.
  Contradiction: Need to cut costs versus need to maintain positive alumni ties.
  Resolution Examples: Automate exit interviews and alumni CRM to maintain ties at low cost.

Examples

Capitalism, general materialism, profit-centred businesses.

Green
Sociocentric

Life is focused around the needs and benefits of a community. Collective values, cooperation and consensus are paramount. Emphasis is on dialogue, relationships and freely chosen affiliations based on shared sentiments. Feelings and caring supersede cold rationality. Equality, diverse points of view and inclusion are prioritised.

Hierarchies are broken down and diverse cultural contexts find common ground, establishing lateral multicultural bonding and linking, and wider networks. Motivated to free society from greed, dogma, selfishness and divisiveness, prioritising feelings, sensitivity and caring. Ecology is another manifestation of these values. Earth's resources are limited and precious, and should be shared equally among everyone.

Characteristics
- Sharing and bonding oriented, building new networks and relationships.
- Ecologically sensitive.
- Tolerant and inclusive.
- Emotional, sensitive and caring.
- Process orientation, communication and dialogue.
- Decentralised and bottom up.

Core Values
Diversity, inclusion, empathetic, bespoke, collaborative, harmony, self-development.

Negative Associations
Appeasing, intangible in nature, focused on emotions rather than reason, loosely structured, time consuming finding common ground.

The Talent Journey through the Green Lens Integrating Ideality and Contradiction Tensions

- **Attraction**
  Ideality: Always inclusive, fair, transparent employer brand and marketing.
  Contradiction: Diversity goals versus efficiency (slower process if balancing both).
  Resolution Example: Blind-screening AI → maintains speed but hides irrelevant data (name, gender).

- **Onboarding**
  Ideality: Always a personalised, empathetic welcome.
  Contradiction: Individual tailoring versus scalability.
  Resolution Example: Hybrid model—AI-curated onboarding with human mentoring circles.

- **Retention**
  Ideality: Always focus on total wellbeing and fairness.
  Contradiction: Productivity demands versus wellbeing (overwork reduces fairness).
  Resolution Example: Predictive analytics to balance workload distribution → prevents burnout while meeting business goals.

- **Leaving**
  Ideality: Dignified, community-focused exit.
  Contradiction: Maintaining ties versus data security (continued alumni contact may risk privacy).
  Resolution Example: Opt-in alumni networks with transparent consent.

Examples
Social enterprises, cooperatives.

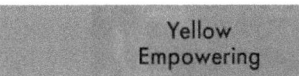

Yellow
Empowering

There is a focus on the individual capacity to expand, develop, discover and overcome limitations, to obtain far-reaching social and individual progress. Imagination is more important than knowledge. The world is seen as a supersystem composed of smaller systems that need to be understood and integrated.

Values of honesty, authenticity and transparency become a direct condition for successful engagement. Experiences override material possessions and the value of immersive enjoyment and intellectual effort becomes paramount. The latter are important as they bring a sense of empowerment as well as freedom of expression, crucial for this value system. Big-picture and systemic thinking are visible manifestations of yellow values.

Characteristics
- Systems thinking.
- Building integrative connections.
- Focused on both process and content.
- Strategic thinking.
- Finding new meaning in ordinary tasks.

Core Values
Strategic, creative, innovative, resourceful, entrepreneurial, transparency and radical honesty, authenticity.

Negative Associations
Difficulty in collaboration with other value systems. Egocentric, impatient, impractically idealistic, work better individually than in teams.

The Talent Journey through the Yellow Lens Integrating Ideality and Contradiction Tensions

- **Attraction**
  Ideality: Always accurate skills-based matching across silos.
  Contradiction: Current job structures versus fluid skills ecosystems.
  Resolution Examples: Run dual approach—maintain role titles (for compliance) while running parallel skills graph.

- **Onboarding**
  Ideality: Fully adaptive integration into knowledge systems.
  Contradiction: Complexity versus clarity (adaptive paths can overwhelm newcomers).
  Resolution Examples: Layered onboarding—simple base modules, with adaptive branching later.

- **Retention**
  Ideality: Friction-free talent fluidly across a boundaryless organisation.
  Contradiction: Manager hoarding versus organisational agility (leaders reluctant to release talent).
  Resolution Examples: Incentivise managers for talent mobility (e.g., 'talent exporter' score).

- **Leaving**
  Ideality: All departing intrinsic knowledge captured, all alumni integrated.
  Contradiction: Knowledge sharing versus confidentiality/IP risk.
  Resolution Examples: Structured offboarding with filtered knowledge capture, anonymised where needed.

Examples
Self-managing organisations coupled with deep purpose.

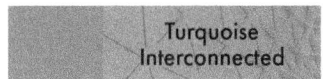

'Life is an evolving interactive whole', experiencing the world as a single, dynamic interdependent organism with its own collective mind. Acknowledging the 'self' as both distinct and a blended part of a larger, compassionate whole.

Motivated to help everything that is alive. Holistic, intuitive thinking and co-operative actions are to be expected. Synthesising science and religion into a universal spirituality.

Characteristics
- Holistic outlook and collective awareness.
- Altruistic—no agenda.
- Integration of methods (instincts, intuition and cognition).
- Seeing the world as an integral whole. Contemplative and compassionate.
- Unity and consensus—global perspectives are combined with local specialist groups.

Core Values
Strive for harmony, unity and consensus to explore, feel and pragmatically work together to solve the large, complex problems to serve humanity and the earth.

Negative Associations
Stay in a spiritual paradigm. May delay pragmatic action.

The Talent Journey through the Turquoise Lens Integrating Ideality and Contradiction Tensions

- **Attraction**

  Ideality: Fully purpose-driven, always mission-aligned talent.

  Contradiction: Global mission versus local needs (planetary purpose may conflict with local economic concerns).

  Resolution Examples: Localise the purpose narrative—same mission expressed in culturally relevant terms.

- **Onboarding**

  Ideality: Full purpose + total wellbeing immersion.

  Contradiction: Universal mission versus personal meaning (not everyone resonates in same way).

  Resolution Examples: AI-guided personalisation of purpose narrative (tailored to personal values).

- **Retention**

  Ideality: Total alignment with global good, balanced with personal growth.

  Contradiction: Sustainability efforts versus short-term profit (tension in resourcing).

  Resolution Examples: Dual metrics dashboards (profit + impact KPIs) so employees see trade-offs transparently.

- **Leaving**

  Ideality: Lifelong stewards and advocates.

  Contradiction: Alumni community versus independence (ex-employees may not want ongoing link).

  Resolution Examples: Voluntary opt-in alumni ecosystem, positioned as global impact movement, not corporate 'control'.

Examples

Buckminster Fuller ideas of spaceship earth and synergetics.

Equaliser Descriptions

Workforce	Description	Left	Right
Value	**The value—both monetary and non-monetary—that employers provide to their employees and broader workforce (temps, contractors, etc.)** Dialling more to the left means more of a focus on a basic package, generic across most employees. Dialling more to the right means a more fully designed, connected employer value proposition focused on multiple elements, designed and customised with different types of employees in mind, fully integrated into the business, aligned to internal employee engagement and brand and external employer marketing and brand strategies.	Package	Proposition
Career	**The functional, emotional and social journeys that candidates and employees go on through their entire careers** Dialling more to the left means several point interventions or initiatives across some parts of the talent journey. Dialling more to the right means greater focus on fully designed, purposeful and experiential talent journeys from pool, interest to attraction, recruitment and retention across different worker types.	Trip	Journey

Workforce	Description	Left	Right
Blend	**The level and mix of diverse workforce models being used strategically for value creation** Dialling more to the left means a greater focus and preference towards permanent work types with a limited mix. Dialling more to the right means strategically harnessing a mix of employment types across permanent, contractors, suppliers, consultants, partners, SOW (statement of work), gig, pay-by-the-hour workers, fractional leaders to tap into new skills, diversity, innovation and more.	Mono	Poly
Belonging	**The integration of diversity and inclusiveness practices across thinking and doing** Dialling more to the left means several point interventions and programmes in relation to legal aspects of diversity. Dialling more to the right means the full integration of the multiple layers of diversity and inclusive thinking and design across leadership, employee and team engagement, strategies, products, services, experiences, projects, operations and brand linked to key business outcomes and indicators.	Inclusion	Integration
Structure	**The levels of bureaucracy at an organisational level** Dialling more to the left means more of a traditional structural model. Referred to most frequently as hierarchical. Or variation of hierarchy, like 'The Matrix'. Dialling more to the right means more formal decentralisation of decision-making authority across the organisation. A focus on flatter structures with fewer levels.	Tall	Flat

Workforce	Description	Left	Right
Learning	**The approaches taken to learning and development** Dialling more to the left means a focus on blended learning and development. Formal structures and learning paths. Some level of customisation. Dialling more to the right means full integration of multimodal, experiential, personalised, on-demand learning and development across all learning channels. Rich media and trans media. Fully utilising enabling technologies like VR/AR and AI.	**Blended**	**Multi**
Skills	**The skills-first orientation of an organisation** Dialling more to the left means a focus on more traditional role-based approaches and role-based design and delivery. Dialling more to the right means a move away from job titles, hierarchies or credentials towards skills-based talent practices across hiring, mobility, development and performance. Supported by strong skills intelligence and a more dynamic approach to work design linking macro, micro and nano projects with skills. Skills realms not job roles.	**Roles**	**Realms**

Workplace	Description	Left	Right
Multiverse	**The degree of merging of physical, digital and virtual places** Dialling more to the left means use of physical place in combination with elements of digital place. Dialling more to the right means a merging of physical, digital and virtual places, optimising each for different types of worktasks (designing, engaging, learning, delivering) and utilising the unique functionalities and opportunities that each place affords.	Place	Metaplace
Experiential	**The extent to which place has been designed from an experience-first perspective** Dialling more to the left means that place has been designed from a functional perspective. Mostly utilitarian with some elements of useful design. Dialling more to the right means having a more experiential workplace across physical, digital and virtual realms, focused on the user and their different needs, linked to the values, goals and essence of the organisation. Focused on the psychological, emotional and sensory design to engage and empower.	Location	Destination

Workplace	Description	Left	Right
	The overall level of flexibility in terms of location, proximity and presence		
Presence	Dialling more to the left means limited level of flexibility in terms of location of work. Work is predominantly conducted in core physical locations or spoke/satellite locations. Some home/third place. Presence is linked to physicality. Dialling to the right means 'flexibility first' and fully integrated. A big focus on all forms of flexible working and practices. Presence not linked mainly to physicality. Remote working practices might be the primary or only way of working. Work can be delivered equally from any place using sophisticated technologies. All supporting elements are optimised for flexibility.	**Fixed**	**Full-Flex**

Worktask	Description	Left	Right
Mindset	**The breadth and depth of thinking in leading, designing and delivering** Dialling more to the left means adopting a mindset that is likely unconsciously partial and biased. Dialling more to the right means purposefully adopting a mindset that integrates human, societal and technological thinking and skills across leading people, designing anything and how work gets delivered. From greyscale to technicolour.	Partial	Holistic
Insight	**The reach and richness of data and insights to make informed decisions** Dialling more to the left means a more reactive, disjointed approach to insights used to support decision making. Dialling more to the right means having a real-time, proactive and predictive pulse across people, processes, products and planet based on qual and quant data.	Disconnected	Predictive
Methods	**The models and methods used to deliver work, value and outcomes** Dialling more to the left means a focus on a limited number of fixed methods and models. Dialling more to the right means utilising a mixed toolbox appropriate to various contexts, colleagues and challenges. More focus on enabling agile thinking and doing. Integration of human-centred models and methods (e.g., design, psychology, anthropology).	Fixed	Adaptive

Worktask	Description	Left	Right
Human–Machine	**The integration of autonomous technologies across organisation tasks** Dialling more to the left means a use primarily of human–machine augmentation and some autonomous activities across a selection of tasks. Dialling more to the right means fully harnessing autonomous task completion using AI autonomous technologies across the full spectrum of strategic, tactical, operational and personal tasks and reshaping the human role in that context.	Human	Autonomous
Empowerment	**The scope of personal empowerment and self-direction delegated to teams and team members** Dialling more to the left means a more traditional leader-directed team model with small to some levels of team empowerment. Dialling more to the right means greater team autonomy over targets and goal setting, team strategy and direction setting, skills development and how work is resourced and delivered by the team.	Leader-Directed	Self-Directed
Value Chain	**The level of responsible and circular practices integrated across the organisation value chain** Dialling more to the left means a primarily efficiency/cost/quality approach whilst fulfilling minimum legal requirements relating to sustainability practices fulfilled. Dialling more to the right means adopting primarily a circular, integrated responsible business approach using these practices as critical jumping-off points for innovation and transformation.	Linear	Circular

Value Impact Matrices

Workforce

	Value			Career			Blend			Belonging		
	-	=	+	-	=	+	-	=	+	-	=	+
Attraction		=			=			=			=	
Retention		=			=			=			=	
Diversity		=			=			=			=	
Sustainability		=			=			=			=	
Efficiency		=			=			=			=	
Belonging		=			=			=			=	
Innovation		=			=			=			=	
Wellbeing		=			=			=			=	
Cost		=			=			=			=	

	Structure			Learning			Skills		
	-	=	+	-	=	+	-	=	+
Attraction		=			=			=	
Retention		=			=			=	
Diversity		=			=			=	
Sustainability		=			=			=	
Efficiency		=			=			=	
Belonging		=			=			=	
Innovation		=			=			=	
Wellbeing		=			=			=	
Cost		=			=			=	

Workforce Aggregate Scores		
-	=	+

Workplace

	Multiverse			Experiential			Presence		
Attraction	-	=	+	-	=	+	-	=	+
Retention	-	=	+	-	=	+	-	=	+
Diversity	-	=	+	-	=	+	-	=	+
Sustainability	-	=	+	-	=	+	-	=	+
Efficiency	-	=	+	-	=	+	-	=	+
Belonging	-	=	+	-	=	+	-	=	+
Innovation	-	=	+	-	=	+	-	=	+
Wellbeing	-	=	+	-	=	+	-	=	+
Cost	-	=	+	-	=	+	-	=	+

Workplace Aggregate Scores		
-	=	+

Worktask

	Mindset			Insight			Methods		
Attraction	-	=	+	-	=	+	-	=	+
Retention	-	=	+	-	=	+	-	=	+
Diversity	-	=	+	-	=	+	-	=	+
Sustainability	-	=	+	-	=	+	-	=	+
Efficiency	-	=	+	-	=	+	-	=	+
Belonging	-	=	+	-	=	+	-	=	+
Innovation	-	=	+	-	=	+	-	=	+
Wellbeing	-	=	+	-	=	+	-	=	+
Cost	-	=	+	-	=	+	-	=	+

	Human-Machine			Empowerment			Value Chain		
Attraction	-	=	+	-	=	+	-	=	+
Retention	-	=	+	-	=	+	-	=	+
Diversity	-	=	+	-	=	+	-	=	+
Sustainability	-	=	+	-	=	+	-	=	+
Efficiency	-	=	+	-	=	+	-	=	+
Belonging	-	=	+	-	=	+	-	=	+
Innovation	-	=	+	-	=	+	-	=	+
Wellbeing	-	=	+	-	=	+	-	=	+
Cost	-	=	+	-	=	+	-	=	+

Worktask Aggregate Scores		
-	=	+

Workforce

Workforce Continuums

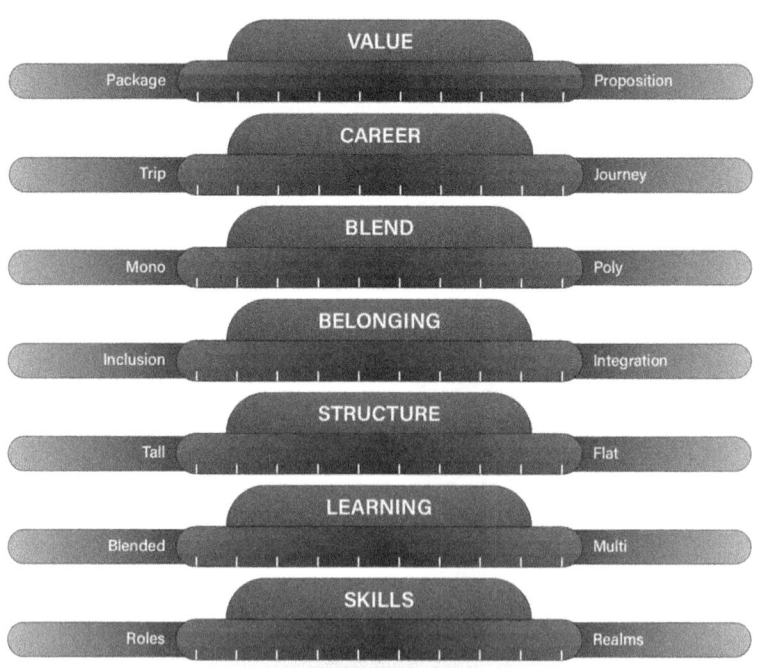

VALUE	Package	Proposition
CAREER	Trip	Journey
BLEND	Mono	Poly
BELONGING	Inclusion	Integration
STRUCTURE	Tall	Flat
LEARNING	Blended	Multi
SKILLS	Roles	Realms

Workforce Continuums

Workplace

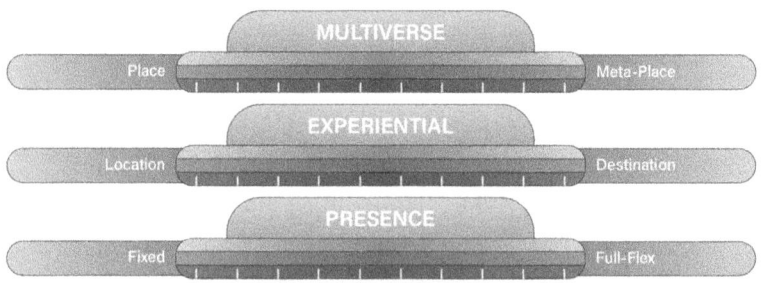

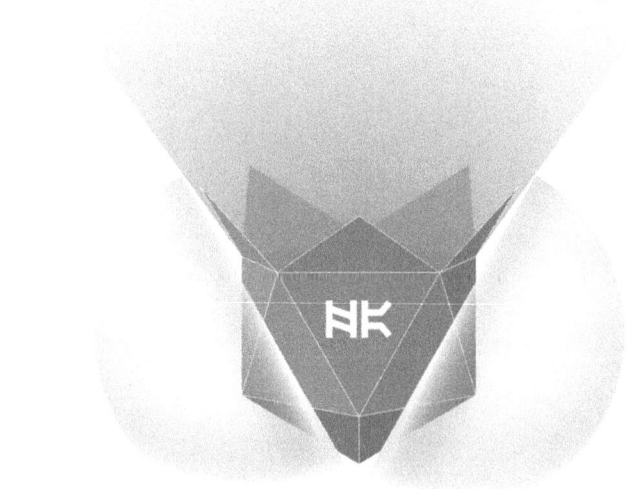

Worktask

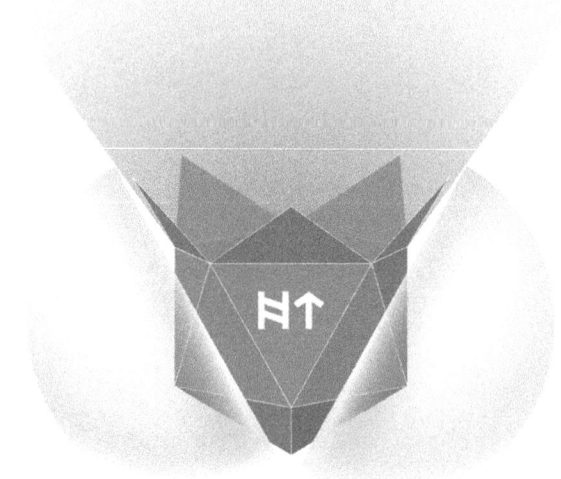

MINDSET
Partial — Holistic

INSIGHT
Disconnected — Predictive

METHODS
Fixed — Adaptive

HUMAN-MACHINE
Human — Autonomous

EMPOWERMENT
Leader-directed — Self-directed

VALUE CHAIN
Linear — Circular

References

Altshuller, G. (1994). And Suddenly the Inventor Appeared: TRIZ, the Theory of Inventive Problem Solving. Technical Innovation Center.

Avdiaj, B., & Ziberi, B. (2019). Job satisfaction, motivation and performance at self-managing teams. International Journal of Economics, Business, and Entrepreneurship, 2(2), 137–154. http://doi.org/10.13140/RG.2.2.15584.64003.

Bar, E., & Boshouwers, S. (2018). Worlds of Wonder: Experience Design for Curious People. BIS Publishers.

Beck, D. E., & Cowan, C. C. (1996). Spiral Dynamics: Mastering Values, Leadership, and Change. Blackwell.

Beck, D. E., Larsen, T. H., Solonin, S., Viljoen, R., & Johns, T. Q. (2018). Spiral Dynamics in Action: Humanity's Master Code. Wiley.

Bersin, J. (2018). AI in HR: The New Frontier. Deloitte Insights.

Blair, R. (2023). Perk's Post-Pandemic Office Design. https://www.perk.com/blog/travelperks-post-pandemic-office-design/.

Bloom, N. (2024). Hybrid Work and Productivity: Evidence from a Randomized Trial [Trip.com hybrid work experiment]. Stanford University.

Bowen, H. R. (1953). Social Responsibilities of the Businessman. Harper & Brothers.

Broadblade (n.d.). Circular economy case study [Company report].

Bukowski, C. (1971). Post Office. Black Sparrow Press.

Buurtzorg (n.d.). Dutch self-managed healthcare organization.

Campbell, J. (1949). The Hero with a Thousand Faces. Pantheon Books.

Cammeraat, E., Samek, L., & Squicciarini, M. (2024). Organisational capital, skills and productivity. Review of Income and Wealth, 70(4).

Celestin, M., & Vanitha, N. (2023). AI VS Hr: Will artificial intelligence replace Human resource professionals?' In 10th International Conference on Multidisciplinary Research and Modern Education. ICMRME-2023 Proceedings (28 May 2023). ISBN Number: 978-920-5-20241-9. Princeton Press.

Chang, S. (2025). The impact of workforce flexibility on organizational operations: Promoting productive employment. Journal of Lifestyle and SDGs Review, 5(1), e03724. https://doi.org/10.47172/2965-730X.SDGsReview.v5.n01.pe03724.

Channel 4 News (2023, March 3). Interview with Simon LeBon.

Chatzopoulou, E., & de Kiewiet, A. (2021). Millennials' evaluation of corporate social responsibility: The wants and needs of the largest and most ethical generation. Journal of Consumer Behaviour, 20(3). https://doi.org/10.1002/cb.1882.

Christensen, C. M. (1997). The Innovator's Dilemma: When New Technologies Cause Great Firms to Fail. Harvard Business Review Press.

ClearStream Goodbody (n.d.). Sustainability consulting firm [Company profile].

Commission on Hybrid and Remote Work (2023). *Hybrid Work Commission 2023.* https://www.publicfirst.co.uk/wp-content/uploads/2023/08/Hybrid-Work-Commission-report-Embargoed-until-13th-Sept-2023.pdf.

Crump, R. (2012). It's Kind of a Cute Story. Bamboo Forest Publishing.

D'Órey, F., Cardoso, A., & Abreu, R. (2019). "Tourist' sense of place", an assessment of the sense of place in tourism studies: The case of Portugal. Academy of Strategic Management Journal, 18(1). http://hdl.handle.net/11328/2722.

De Bruin, J. H., Doodkorte, R. J. P., Sinervo, T., & Clemens, T. (2022). The implementation and outcomes of self-managing teams in elderly care: A scoping review. Journal of Nursing Management, 30(8), 4549–4559. https://doi.org/10.1111/jonm.13836.

Dees, J. G. (n.d.). Writings on social entrepreneurship.

Design Council UK (n.d.). The Double-Diamond Design Process. Design Council.

Dries, N., Luyckx, J., Stephan, U., & Collings, D. G. (2025). The future of work: A research agenda. Journal of Management. https://doi.org/10.1177/01492063251320025.

Duarte, F. (2024). *Number of Freelancers.* https://explodingtopics.com/blog/number-of-freelancers?utm_source=chatgpt.com.

Duran Duran (n.d.). https://duranduran.com.

Eurofound (2024). *Living and Working in Europe.* https://www.eurofound.europa.eu/en/topics/living-and-working-europe.

European Policy Forum (2025). How to ensure a skills-based future for European competitiveness. Intereconomics, 60(1), 11–17.

Fisher, J. C., & Pry, R. H. (1971). A simple substitution model of technological change. Technological Forecasting and Social Change, 3(1), 75–88.

Future of Work Institute (2019). *Future of Work World Whitepaper.* https://landing.cpl.com/future-of-work/future-of-work-world.html.

Future of Work Institute (2021). *Workplace Wellness: Time to Get Strategic.* https://landing.cpl.com/future-of-work/fowi_strategic_wellness_whitepaper.pdf.

Future of Work Institute (2024–2025). *Changing Expectations of Work and Life* [Due October 2025].

Gaelic Athletic Association (n.d.). Organizational structure and cultural practices.

Gartner (2020). AI-Driven HR: Trends and Predictions. Gartner.

Ghorashi, S. (2014). Memenomics: The Next-Generation Economic System. SelectBooks.

GPJ (2022). Cisco's Global Sales Experience (GSX). George P. Johnson Experience Marketing. https://www.gpj.com/case-study/ciscos-global-sales-experience-gsx/.

Graves, C. W. (1970). *Spiral Dynamics* [Unpublished manuscript; later popularised by Beck & Cowan].

Haines, V. Y., Guerrero, S., & Marchand, A. (2024). Flexible work arrangements and employee turnover intentions: Contrasting pathways. International Journal of Human Resource Management, 35(11), 1970–1995. https://doi.org/10.1080/09585192.2024.2323510.

Hall, B. H., Lotti, F. & Mairesse, J. (2013). Evidence on the impact of R&D and ICT investments on innovation and productivity in Italian firms. Economics of Innovation and New Technology, 22(3), 300–328.

Hartijasti, Y., Irawanto, D. W., & Riani, A. L. (2020). Perceived leadership behaviors among multigenerational managers. In *Proceedings of the Global Conference on Business and Social Sciences*.

Hench, J. (2003). Designing Disney: Imagineering and the Art of the Show. Disney Editions.

IDEO (2009). *The Human-Centered Design Toolkit.*

IDEO (2015). *The Field Guide to the Human-Centered Design Kit.*

Isaac Care (n.d.). Connected care platform [Company profile].

Janni, N. (2023). Leader as Healer. LID Publishing.

Jesuthasan, R., & Boudreau, J. W. (2022). Work without Jobs: How to Reboot Your Organization's Work Operating System. MIT Press.

Kano, N. (1984). Attractive quality and must-be quality. The Journal of the Japanese Society for Quality Control, 14(2), 39–48.

Kapp, K. M., & Defelice, R. A. (2019). Microlearning: Short and sweet. American Society for Training and Development.

Kerlin, J. A., & Monroe-White, T. (2016). Social enterprise in the United States and Europe: Understanding and learning from the differences. Voluntas, 27(1), 1625–1642.

Kleon, A. (2014). Show Your Work!: 10 Ways to Share Your Creativity and Get Discovered. Algonquin Books.

Koch, J., & Schermuly, C. C. (2020). Agile project management and sensation seeking: Exploring psychological predictors of agile preferences. Journal of Business Research, 110, 464–474.

Koch, J., & Schermuly, C. C. (2021). Who is attracted and why? How agile project management influences employees' attraction and commitment. International Journal of Managing Projects in Business, 14(3), 699–720. https://doi.org/10.1108/IJMPB-02-2020-0063.

Koivunen, S., Ala-Luopa, S., & Haapakorpi, A. (2022). The march of Chatbots into recruitment: recruiters' experiences, expectations, and design opportunities. Computer Supported Cooperative Work (CSCW), 31(3), 487–516.

Korkis, J. (2011). *On Walt Disney's Love of Miniatures.* https://www.walt disney.org/blog/miniature-worlds-walt.

Kosinowski, G. (2020). Trust in cooperatives. In B. Díaz Díaz, N. Capaldi, S. O. Idowu & R. Schmidpeter (Eds.), Responsible Business in a Changing World (pp. 77–95). Springer.

Kuhn, T. S. (1962). The Structure of Scientific Revolutions. University of Chicago Press.

Laloux, F. (2014). Reinventing Organizations: A Guide to Creating Organizations Inspired by the Next Stage of Human Consciousness. Nelson Parker.

Lego Group (n.d.). Leadership playground [Internal leadership development framework].

LinkedIn (2024). *Workplace Learning Report.* LinkedIn.

Littaye, A., & Ghez, D. (2012). Disneyland Paris: From Sketch to Reality. Neverland Editions.

Louttit, J. (2024). Leading Impactful Teams: Achieving Low-Stress Success in Project Management. De Gruyter.

Lynch, C. (2025). The Assets Ladder. Self Published. https://www.amazon.ie/Assets-Ladder-Learn-More-Earn/dp/1836547455.

Lua Health (n.d.). AI-driven linguistic inference for wellbeing [Company profile].

Luger, M., Hofer, K. M., & Floh, A. (2021/2022). Support for corporate social responsibility among Generation Y consumers in advanced versus emerging markets. International Business Review, 31, 101903.

Malik, P. (2022). *Salesforce gamification: The essential elements for user adoption.* https://www.salesforceben.com/salesforce-gamification-the-essential-elements-for-user-adoption/.

Mann, D. (2002). Hands-on Systematic Innovation. CREAX Press.

Manurung, E. M., Fransiska, F., & Turnawan, A. V. (2024). Virtual world, Metaverse, and Gen Z's social life. Indonesian Journal of Economics, Social and Humanities, 6(2), 153–160, 202.

McKinsey & Co. (2022). AI in HR: Transforming Talent Management. McKinsey.

Misra, K. (2019). Work–life flexibility practices and employee outcomes: Does the cultural context matter? Journal of International Management Studies, 19(1), 27–38. https://doi.org/10.18374/JIMS-19-1.4.

Mondragon Corporation (n.d.). Spanish co-operative federation.

Morikawa, M., Martela, F., & Hakanen, J. (2025) Are employee self-management and organizational self-management related to work engagement or burnout? Evidence from two studies. Business Research Quarterly, 28(2), 386–398.

Narayanan, S. (2022). Does Generation Z value and reward corporate social responsibility practices? Journal of Marketing Management, 38(9–10), 903–937.

Negnevitsky, M. (2025a). The Rise of Autonomous AI Agents: Automating Complex Tasks. University of Tasmania.

Negnevitsky, M. (2025b). Autonomous AI Agents and the Future of Work. AI & Society.

Nurski, L., & Alcidi, C. (2024). *How to ensure a skills-based future for European competitiveness.* CEPS. CEPS contribution to the special series 'The EU's path to 2030'.

Office for National Statistics (2025). UK Remote Work Trends Report. Office for National Statistics.

Ogirri, K. O., & Idugie, I. J. (2024). A comparative analysis of traditional versus agile project management methodologies on IT project outcomes. Asian Journal of Research in Computer Science, 17(9), 1–12. https://doi.org/10.9734/ajrcos/2024/v17i9495.

Orpheus (n.d.). Self-managed orchestra model.

Østergaard, E. K. (2019). Teal Dots in an Orange World. LID Publishing.

Pantelides, A. (2025a). Gen Z concepts of leadership: Formulating archetypes based on inter-relational business, political, and generational characteristics. Athens Journal of Business & Economics, 11, 1–26. https://doi.org/10.30958/ajbe.X-Y-Z.

Pantelides, A. (2025b). Gen Z and the Future of Work: A Democratic Shift. Future Work Studies.

Perez, C. A., Ubierna, F., Arranz, C. F. A., Arroyabe, M. F., & Fernández de Arróyabe, J. C. (2023). The formation of self-management teams in higher education institutions: Satisfaction and effectiveness. Studies in Higher Education, 48(6), 910–925. https://doi.org/10.1080/03075079.2023.2172565.

Pine, B. J. (2024). The Experience Economy: Office as Flagship. Harvard Business Review Press.

Pine, B. J., & Dubois, L.-E. (2024, September 16). The 'flagship office' is on the rise—and it uses the principles of the experience economy to coax employees back to their desks, Fortune. https://fortune.com/2024/09/16/flagship-office-return-experience-economy-employees-remote-in-person-work/.

Pine, B. J., & Gilmore, J. H. (1999). The Experience Economy: Work is Theatre & Every Business a Stage. Harvard Business Review Press.

Rajaram, H., & Jha, A. M. (2024). The impact of flexible work arrangements on job satisfaction. International Journal for Research in Applied Science and Engineering Technology, 12(III). https://doi.org/10.22214/ijraset.2024.59265.

Rani, S., & Suneja, A. (2025). Attracting talent: Understanding Generation Z's expectations of technology-driven workplaces. VILAKSHAN – XIMB Journal of Management. https://doi.org/10.1108/XJM-08-2024-0129.

Rank, S., & Contreras, F. (2021). Do Millennials pay attention to Corporate Social Responsibility in comparison to previous generations? Are they motivated to lead in times of transformation? A qualitative review of generations, CSR and work motivation. International Journal of Corporate Social Responsibility, 6(4). https://doi.org/10.1186/s40991-020-00058-y.

Rogers, E. M. (1962). Diffusion of Innovations. Free Press.

Sawicka, J. (2023). Environmental CSR and the purchase declarations of Generation Z. Sustainability, 15(17), 12759.

Spiegler, S. V., Heinecke, C., & Wagner, S. (2021). An empirical study on changing leadership in agile teams. Empirical Software Engineering, 26 (41). https://doi.org/10.1007/s10664-021-09949-5.

Spotify (n.d.). Agile squad-based structure.

Suyanto, S., & Anggreani, M. P. (2025). Navigating Conscious Unbossing: Understanding Gen Z's Reluctance Towards Traditional Leadership Roles. International Commission on Missing Persons.

Suzuki, S. (1970). Zen Mind, Beginner's Mind. Weatherhill.

The Economic Times (2025, June 21). Blue-collar gig hiring jumps 92% in 2024, led by e-commerce and delivery platforms: Report. The Economic Times. https://economictimes.indiatimes.com/jobs/hr-policies-trends/blue-collar-gig-hiring-jumps-92-in-2024-led-by-e-commerce-and-delivery-platforms-report/articleshow/121992503.cms?utm_source=chatgpt.com.

The Guardian (2025, January 27). Inequality in flexible working dividing Britain into 'two-tier workforce'. The Guardian. https://www.theguardian.com/money/2025/jan/27/inequality-in-flexible-working-dividing-britain-into-two-tier-workforce.

The Transformation Architects (n.d.). Workplacemaking. https://www.thetransformationarchitects.com/workplacemaking.html.

Thomke, S. H. (2020). Experimentation Works: The Surprising Power of Business Experiments. Harvard Business Review Press.

Tupper, H. (2020). The Squiggly Career. Portfolio Penguin.

Utopia (1981–1986). Nordic research project on trade union-based development of, and training in, computer technology and work organization.

Valdés-Flores, P., & Campos-Rodríguez, J. A. (2011). Personal skills, job satisfaction, and productivity in members of high-performance teams. College Teaching Methods & Styles Journal, 4(1), 81–86. https://doi.org/10.19030/CTMS.V4I1.5052.

Vancauwenberghe, B. (2025, March 30). *Why digital are reshaping Generation Z & Alpha identity.* https://www.20something.be/why-digital-are-reshaping-generation-z-alpha-identity/.

Webber, A. L. (2018). Unmasked: The Autobiography of the Musical Theatre Legend. Harper Collins.

Winsor, J., & Paik, Jin H. (2024). Open Talent. Harvard Business Review Press. ISBN 9781647823887.

World Economic Forum (2020). Reports on New Capitalism and the Future of Work. World Economic Forum.

World Economic Forum (2024). Human-Centred AI for Human Resources Professionals. World Economic Forum.

Youth Forum Europe (2023). Digital belonging among European teens.

Interviews (and Thanks to)

Ger Corbett, CEO, Sandyford Business District

Dr Angie Nagle, Co-Founder, Bladebridge

Dr Declan Bogan, Head of Sustainability Learning and Training, Goodbody Clearstream

Suzanne Dolan, MD, Covalen Outsourcing Solutions

John Twomey, MD, Flexsource Solutions

Ben Mason, CEO, Global Bridge

James Louttit, Founder, Impactful Project Management

Elysia Hegarty, Assistant Director, Future of Work Institute

Paul Conneally, CEO, Slick+

Geoffrey Allen, CEO, Mersus Technologies

Raj Bhalla, CEO, Fortal Virtual Workspaces

Noemi Alvarez, CEO, Insight Sphere

Conor Lynch, Founder and CEO, Career Lab

Josephine Kelliher (from FWW vlog), Arts Experiences and Curation

Other Featured Companies with Interaction

Lua Health—Founder, Mihael Arcan
Isaac Care—CEO Declan Murphy

Albums Mentioned in the Book You Need to Listen to (Ideally When Reading This Book)

The Doors, The Doors 1967
Jesus Christ Superstar (original recording), Tim Rice and Andrew Lloyd Weber 1971
Tapestry, Carole King 1971
Led Zeppelin IV, Led Zeppelin 1971
Dirty Mind, Prince 1980
Rio, Duran Duran 1982

Index